HOOKERS, MIDGETS, AND FIRE TRUCKS

An Invitation to Our Party

LINDA GAYLE THOMPSON

iUniverse, Inc.
New York   Bloomington

Hookers, Midgets, and Fire Trucks
An Invitation to Our Party

iUniverse books may be ordered through booksellers or by contacting:

iUniverse
1663 Liberty Drive
Bloomington, IN 47403
www.iuniverse.com
1-800-Authors (1-800-288-4677)

ISBN: 978-1-4401-9834-2 (pbk)
ISBN: 978-1-4401-9833-5 (cloth)
ISBN: 978-1-4401-9836-6 (ebk)

Printed in the United States of America

Library of Congress Control Number: 2010913484

iUniverse rev. date: 10/5/2010

Warning Label

As you can see from the title, this book is politically incorrect and quite possibly offensive to some or even most. For that reason, I felt it necessary to begin with a warning and an apology.

Our family, although not completely normal by most people's standards, is real, and the events that unfold are true. Some names and locations have been changed to protect the privacy of the not so innocent.

My apologies to all prostitutes, little people, and firefighters if you find the title offensive. As you will discover in the pages of this book, you are exceptionally near and dear to my heart, and no malice was intended in the role you play in our wacky world.

Disclaimer

The nutritional and medical advice mentioned within the pages of this book is either anecdotal or being passed along to you from my own readings. While all the books mentioned are included in the resources, I am not a doctor or a medical professional and cannot vouch for the accuracy of medical information. Always consult your own doctor or a healthcare or nutrition specialist about your individual situation or concerns.

Acknowledgment

When I think of all the people who helped in the creation of *Hookers, Midgets, and Fire Trucks*, I am so appreciative of my editors. First, I thank Peggy Stautberg, who got me on the right track. To Aabha Brown and Heather Watkins, your input was invaluable. Aabha, thanks for helping me search my soul. To all my friends and family who read all or parts of the book and gave me both criticism and encouragement, I am indebted.

Thank you to the most wonderful son-in-law and smartest man in the world, Chris Travis. The cover rocks! I thank my Creator every day for your wisdom, sense of humor, and the fact that you are my daughter's husband and the father of my grandchildren. Our whole world is better because we have you.

Thank you to my sister, Denise King, for helping me share our story. If even one person is helped from the writing of *Hookers, Midgets, and Fire Trucks,* we will not have walked our path in vain.

Thank you, Hailey Williams, for your creative genius and outstanding work on my Web site. Auntie Linda thinks you are amazing.

I am so fortunate to have met Scott Corron, my photographer, fellow seeker, and all-around wonderful person. Scott, you did a super job for me. You and your extraordinary experiences have enriched my life.

Lynn Williams, also known as Tammye Toe, my sister-in-law, this acknowledgment would not have been complete without mentioning the person who introduced me to Mike. Thank you, sweetie … what a ride!

I would like to take this opportunity to thank Dwan Coleman for being the best friend Mike could have ever had. Thanks, Dwan, for your unwavering support. Mike loved you with all his heart. I appreciate you more than words can explain.

Denis and Diana, how could we have possibly made it without you? The blocks under Mike's wheelchair tires were a little cold, Denis. Sorry about the leather coat!

To my Ruthie Beaman, best friend, co-conspirator, and laugh machine: thanks for your unyielding support, for believing in me no matter what, and because you let me use you and supplements as my personal science experiment.

Tiffany Lynn Travis, my editor, my task master, my critical genius—your input made our story! You have been a pain in the ass, my publicist, my friend, my daughter, and my champion. I am amazed at your talent, tenacity, brilliance, and beauty (inside and out). I have been so blessed that you have made this trip with me. I love you, Mom.

CONTENTS

Prologue

Since I believe that life, love, laughter, pain, and sorrow are our best teachers, I would like to share with you my life filled with both the highest highs and the lowest lows. This journey on earth has given me love beyond compare and has sent me spiritual soul mates with whom I have shared so much joy and laughter that I am sure no human being could be more blessed than I.

I have also spent eighteen of the toughest years of my life as the caregiver for a quadriplegic husband, followed by one catastrophic blow after another. Grief has been an important part of my destiny.

It is when we reach the bottom that we receive the gift of learning the greatest lessons. Clinical depression and the events that gave it birth sent me on a desperate quest. My spiritual growth and firsthand experience with miracles and angels are a direct result of my darkest hours. I was reborn with the understanding that I am wonderful, you are wonderful, we are all one, and happiness is attainable even in the midst of life's worst challenges.

As you will see in the following pages, pretty much all of my life lessons I have learned the hard way—by plunging in headfirst! But I've come out on the other side of so many difficult, and just as often joyful, experiences, that the lessons I've learned are deeply felt and universal enough that I want to share them within the pages of this book.

To the millions of you who struggle with depression or know people who do, I have traveled that hard road; it is my hope that by reading about my path back to joy, you may find some answers for yourself or someone you love. It is also my fervent desire that if you have lost a loved one, you will glean hope from the miracles I share and perhaps even seek a miracle of your own.

At this point, many of you may be wondering, "What do hookers, midgets, and fire trucks have to do with depression, grief, and spirituality? Is this just one woman's ramblings, or is it comedy, spirituality, tragedy, satire, or smut?" You see, in my life, it's actually all of the above. I've learned you never know what or who life is going to bring to the party.

To all of you who are seekers of truth, love, and laugher, I give you the story of a family, my life, and the lessons I have learned along the way. This is your invitation to our party.

CHAPTER 1
LINDA, THE BEGINNING

I WAS BORN LINDA GAYLE KING on August 14, 1949. It was a time of innocence. Ed Sullivan was the hit on television, but we didn't have a TV. Perry Como crooned the beautiful love ballad "Some Enchanted Evening" on the radio. We never heard a four-letter word. The new toy was Silly Putty—no sex or violence there. Did the censorship help us or hurt us? I don't know. What I do know is that I was born with the great fortune of having parents and grandparents who loved me, and our home was usually filled with fun and laughter. Even considering their human qualities, mistakes and all, as far as earthly angels are concerned, I attribute much of my joy to my parents, Warren and Bessie King, and to my paternal grandmother, Lola Olivia King, whom I called "Granny." I vividly remember sitting on Granny's sunny front porch at age eight with giant purple hydrangeas in the flowerbed beside me, and it occurred to me: *I am the happiest person on earth.*

We were a typical middle-class family in the fifties. My parents, who both worked for the Southern Pacific Railroad, were raising two kids in a modest home in Bellaire, Texas. My sister, Denise, with her beautiful, dark brown ringlet hair and large, expressive hazel eyes, came along almost seven years after me. Our life was golden—which had nothing to do with money. Mama quit working when I was three, and although Daddy never missed a day's work, I can still remember Mama saying, "Eeney meeny miney moe," letting fate decide which bills got paid each month. Even in a golden world where the happiest person on earth resides, innocence has a way of slipping away when no one is looking.

It was September of 1961, and Hurricane Carla was in the Gulf. The ceiling fan in the hall sucked air in through the windows that were cracked open one or two inches all over the house. It was hot and humid. The wind was blowing hard, dark clouds rumbled, and lightning streaked across the sky.

Daddy, Mama, their friends, Jerry and Maddy, Denise, and I were watching the weather. The Citizen's Band (CB) radio droned and buzzed its alerts. The small, white three-bedroom, one-bath frame house we had been living in from the time I was born creaked with the onslaught of wind.

I was twelve, a really gawky, skinny girl, stuck in that awkward in-between stage, but I was mostly kid, still innocent. I did everything I was told, respected my elders, said "yes, sir" and "no, ma'am," and above all never questioned anything Mama and Daddy ever said. Maybe that's why I wasn't frightened as I peeked through the venetian blinds to see garbage cans flying down the street of our neighborhood, which included lots of other small, wood-framed houses. My parents weren't worried about the storm. Why should I be? Heck, they were playing cards with their friends.

Jerry stretched his arms, leaned back in his chair, and said in an annoyed tone, "Y'all mind if I move that CB to the back? I can barely hear myself think." The other three adults nodded in agreement and continued arranging their cards. Our house only had a small kitchen, a dining room open to the equally small living room, where the bridge game was being played, a hall, and three tiny bedrooms. Jerry moved the CB to the middle bedroom, Denise's room, and closed the door as he came back to join the game.

Slanted, driving rain battered the windows, and Mama looked up from her card game to see the hardwood floors getting wet. "Girls, go around and close all the windows, and then, Denise Kaye, it's eight o'clock—time for bed." I was older, so I got to stay up till ten.

Denise whined her usual complaint, "Why do I have to go to bed and Linda gets to stay up?"

"Because I said so." Mama's response never varied from one night to the next, but I guess when you're five you still have to give it your best shot. Mama never vacillated and came out the victor every time. Denise and I closed the windows. She gave hugs and kisses to our parents and then the customary "I love yous" were exchanged. I marched her back to bed to tuck her in.

Seven years is a pretty big age difference. I always felt more like Denise's mother than her sister. The CB radio crackled. I turned the volume down. As I pulled the covers over Denise's chest, she pleaded, "Linda, please let me sleep with you tonight."

"Denise, you know there's nothin' to be afraid of. Carla's a long way away—all the way to Galveston."

"No, Linda, it's not that. I just don't want to sleep by myself tonight. I won't pee the bed, I promise."

"Denise, you say that every time, and every time you pee all over me."

"No, really, Linda, Mama just gave me honey. I won't pee tonight. It helps. It really does."

"Denise, I'm not sleepin' in a wet bed tonight. Now go to sleep." I turned off the light, walked out, and closed the door.

Mama served chips and Cokes. The card game continued, and Jerry got up occasionally to get updates on Carla. The wind howled. Denise got out of bed several times and got in big trouble.

Daddy stepped in, saying, "Denise, you get out of bed again and you're gonna get a whippin'."

Daddy and Jerry won a game, and the ladies shuffled and dealt. Jerry got up and went into Denise's room.

Denise yelled, "Linda, come 'ere!"

Daddy and I exchanged glances. "It's okay, Daddy, I'll check and see what she needs. Maybe she's scared of the wind."

I walked into Denise's room and flipped on the light. Jerry was in the corner, kneeling down by the CB. Denise was in her bed. The static from the storm update crackled. Denise's huge hazel eyes were filled with raw fear. She threw her arms around my neck and whispered, begging, "Linda, please don't leave me."

Instant recognition of totally blocked memories flashed like the lightning outside. I was five. Jerry was carrying me on his back. His finger slipped into my panties, innocent tiny girl panties, and probed. Oh my god! How could I have forgotten? Now she was his victim too. Denise's and my eyes locked.

"I won't leave you, baby girl," I said as I unwound her arms from my neck. I stood up, turned around, faced the monster, and found fury.

Jerry stood looking at me, and I saw he knew I knew. He was afraid I was going to tell, and I was glad he was afraid. With a voice that could not possibly have come from me, an innocent, I said with quiet, fiery hate and without a doubt, "If you ever touch her again, I will kill you. Get the hell out." He left.

I set the CB radio out in the hall, flipped off the light, closed the door, and climbed in bed with my little sister. "I'm so sorry, Denise. I'm so sorry, baby girl. I'm so, so sorry." We were both crying quietly. We were good girls, polite. We had been taught to protect the monster.

Through the closed door, I heard voices in the living room and Mama telling them they couldn't possibly go out with the wind blowing like it was. And then I heard the front door close. I knew he was gone.

I was on my side, facing Denise. She turned with her back to me, snuggled close, and drew my arm around her. We spooned and fell asleep. In the early morning hours, Hurricane Carla raged wildly outside, but I felt really warm. And then I felt really cold. The honey didn't work.

The following morning, the storm still raged, and I knew Daddy didn't have to go to work. I woke up before Denise, got out of my damp clothes, and showered. My mind raced. It seemed impossible to me that I had totally forgotten, completely blocked the bad memories of a family friend who had touched me on my privates. I wondered what he did to my little sister. The monster had to be stopped. My parents would know what to do. I had to tell them, and they would see that he was punished.

Denise was still sleeping. I went to Mama and Daddy's room. Their door was open, and they were still in bed but not asleep. I walked in and closed the door. I knew without a doubt my parents loved me, and they loved Denise too. They said it. They showed it. And they meant it.

I felt strong. I was doing the right thing. I began my story.

"When I was little, Jerry put his hands on me. Then I forgot all about it. Now he's doin' it to Denise."

Mama and Daddy's horror was plain to see. Daddy's face was a combination of rage and compassion. He questioned, "Linda, what did he actually do to you?"

"Not much. When I sat down at the piano, he sat next to me and put his hand on my leg …" I couldn't do it. I couldn't tell *all* he had done to me, shoving his finger in me. My mother's response was not what I expected. Her voice was almost shrill.

"Linda Gayle, why didn't you tell us? If you told us, Denise wouldn't have had to go through it!"

My response was short—"I know."

Daddy softened the blow, saying, "Baby, your mother and I need to talk about this."

In my twelve-year-old mind, we had just summed it up. Denise had been molested, and it was my fault. As I left their room and closed the door, Denise walked out of her room.

"I'm sorry I peed on you, Linda."

"It's okay." I shrugged.

Mama and Daddy didn't often argue, and never in front of us. We could hear their muffled voices coming from behind their door. I ushered Denise into the kitchen and made us both a bowl of cereal.

About an hour later, our parents called us into their room. Daddy called Denise over to him and gave her a hug. "Linda told us what Jerry has been doin' to you. If a man ever tries to touch you again, you kick the hell out of him as hard as you can right here." Daddy demonstrated by putting his hand over his crotch. "Got it?" Denise giggled and nodded she understood. He continued, "Mama and I have been talkin', and we have decided not to do anything about this because if we took him to court you girls would be dragged through the mud."

Mama chimed in, "And we have to remember Maddy's feelings."

At the time I didn't question their decision. I never questioned anything they ever said. The monster got away.

My insecurities began early. It's a common side effect of molested children. But there was more. Isn't it weird and horrifying how children attach themselves to negativity? My father, who was incredibly kind, generous, loving, and funny, teased me by calling me his "dumb kid." Back then, calling your child dumb or worse was commonplace. Daddy would also tell me to show people my feet. He said they were the eighth wonder of the world. I had long, skinny, big feet. I laughed a lot with him about the feet. I didn't laugh about the dumb kid part.

Words, even when said in fun and with no malicious intent, can be like the crushing blows of fists, especially to a child. Adults would do well to censor every word said to a child before it exits their mouth.

Unfortunately, I believed my dad. Even though hurting me in any way was the last thing Daddy would have intentionally done to me, that belief—that I was dumb—and the sexual trauma I experienced as a child became the basis for most of my insecurities. I was well into my thirties before I realized I was an intelligent human being.

Being a "dumb kid," I hated school. I was in the Yellow Bird reading group. There were Red Birds and Blue Birds, and then the "dumb kids" were in the Yellow Bird group. To make matters worse, my first grade teacher was evil. She terrified me, spanking my hands with a ruler and humiliating me in front of the class when I couldn't read as well as the others. School was agonizing for me, but somehow I managed to survive grade school and junior high, and then in my sophomore year of high school, Daddy and Mama decided to move to Lufkin, where they bought a tract of land deep in the Piney Woods of East Texas. The thirty-five acres they bought had a small wood-frame house on it, a place for us to live while they built a new home.

Having grown up in the big city, I realized I was a country girl at heart. Helping Daddy with a garden, making homemade cream corn with our new neighbors and even baling hay all came as natural to me as breathing. At age fifteen I could feel a positive change taking place in me. Maybe it was watching things grow, the fresh air, or maybe I was just reaching puberty late...Whatever it was, I know I felt at home.

· · · · ·

LINDA'S LESSONS

Over the years I learned that molested children often have a difficult time talking about what happened to them and it is very common for them to block memories of their abuse. After sixty years of carrying the guilt of being the cause of my sister's molestation, I am finally able to lay it to rest.

Thinking back on my experiences in first grade, I remember mostly fear. School should be a place children feel safe and motivated in a positive way. To most of the world's teachers who inspire, love, and create a positive atmosphere in the classroom for all students equally, I commend you. The world owes you a huge debt, which should be given to you in the form of respect, honor and at least double the salary!

Chapter 2
A Growth Spurt

Lufkin is where I "got religion." Our family had attended church a few times while we lived in Bellaire, but we always just stopped going. When we moved to Lufkin, I was drawn to the tiny, white-frame church just up the road from our house.

I attended the first Sunday by myself, and afterward Daddy confided in me, "You know, baby girl, I promised God if he would help me get a place in the country, I'd start goin' to church. Can I go with you the next week?"

That was the beginning of how our family became Baptist. Mama, Daddy, Denise, and I would load up in the car on Sunday morning and head for church, and Mama would begin her lecture, saying, "Now, listen, all three of you, if you get tickled in church again I'm gonna stop coming with y'all. It's embarrassing."

Denise's response was always outright giggling, but Daddy, who always drove, would peek back at me in the rearview mirror and wink. He and I would both restrain our smiles, and then I would say, "Yes, ma'am."

And he would say, "Yes, ma'am."

And then Denise would laugh and say, "Yes, ma'am."

I guess laughing is not something a person normally associates with going to church, but we went to a wonderful, special church. The Berryhill Baptist Church had its characters. Aunt Fanny would pray, and when I say pray, I mean for fifteen minutes or longer every time. Everyone in the church was always relieved when the preacher asked Aunt Fanny to pray when we were sitting down. Of course, that was bad too, because the seventy-year-old deacon, Hardy, who sat right up front on the left side of the church, would always fall asleep when Aunt Fanny got to praying. When Hardy fell asleep, he would start snoring. Aubrey, the deacon who became our good friend, sat right behind Hardy and was baldheaded. When Hardy started snoring, Aubrey's bald spot would turn red, which meant that he was tickled and trying to keep from laughing. When Aubrey's bald spot turned red, there was no hope for Daddy and me. I always sat next to Daddy, and when I could feel him shaking and laughing with no sound, I was done for. Mama always leaned forward and took on the look that meant, *You two are in so much trouble.* And of course that made the whole thing that much funnier.

So many funny things happened at church. One summer Sunday when it was over one hundred degrees outside, we had a full house. Berryhill Baptist had no air conditioning. There was going to be a picnic on the grounds following the service. Oh, the food those country ladies cooked was good. Inside, though, the temperature was probably close to a hundred. Fans stirred the hot air around, but we were all still sweating. The only protection we had from the bright sunlight was some very old, very yellowed roll-up shades on the windows. Our little family always sat on the left side about three rows behind Aubrey. Jimmy, five years old, was the worst little hellion in the church, and he sat with his family right behind Hardy, who sat by himself in the front row. Hardy had earned his place of distinction due to his age and years of service. All was well on this day until the sun started blaring through the window next to Hardy, sort of blinding him. The preacher had built his sermon to a fever pitch and was bringing it back down a notch or two so that it was relatively quiet in the church. Hardy began to slide quietly across the pew to rectify the bright sun situation. When he reached the end of the pew, Jimmy now sat directly behind him. With the utmost quiet, Hardy stood up, bent over, and reached for the shade. At the same time, Jimmy jumped up onto his seat, leaned over the front pew, and goosed Hardy right between his butt cheeks. Hardy bolted straight up in the air. It seemed that his sphincter muscle connected to his hands, because he grabbed the shade and ripped it off the wall.

When he landed on his feet again, he whirled around and before the whole church shouted, "You little son of a bitch!" Aubrey's bald spot turned red, and Daddy and I were uncontrollable. Mama actually stayed out of church the next week, but then she forgave us.

The stories about the Berryhill Baptist Church could fill a whole other book. We met the most wonderful people there, and eventually Daddy, Aubrey, and countless others joined together and built a beautiful new brick sanctuary, air conditioning and all.

Church wasn't all silliness and laughter to me. It actually became a very serious part of my life. The sermons we heard were about Jesus and love, but also about hell, fire, and brimstone. I became really worried for my family and friends and then everyone. Who was going to hell and why? I walked down the aisle and asked Jesus to be my savior. Mama, Daddy, and Denise followed close behind. I knocked on doors and solicited converts. Fear was my motivating factor.

By this time, I was finishing high school. I was a nerdy kid who made Cs and was pretty much in the background of all the school functions. I had a couple of serious boyfriends, but my eye was on college. As much as I hated school, there was nothing I wouldn't do to not let my parents down. Mama had her high school diploma, but Daddy only had a ninth-grade education, and it was their dream for me to be a college graduate.

After high school, I went on to attend college at Stephen F. Austin State University in Nacogdoches, just thirty miles north of Lufkin. Mama thought it would be good for my social adjustment if I lived in the dorm. I had also been dating a guy who was four years older than me, and I'm sure that was her main motivation in sending me away. I still remember the day I left. Daddy was an avid reader, and he had just read a story in *Time* magazine about the high rate of suicide among college freshmen. Daddy was also an avid eater. He loved food, and so his advice to me as I left for college was, "Baby girl, no matter how bad it gets over there, you can always go eat a hamburger." He was grinning, red-faced, and tears ran down his cheeks, unashamed.

Mama stood beside him crying too. "Warren, does it always have to be about food with you?" Mama didn't get it, but I did. No matter what you have to face or how hard the moment may be, a little humor always helps. I gained twenty pounds my freshman year.

College was the beginning of socialization for me. I think I was just one of those people who found it easier to be an adult than a child. Dorm life was a hoot. Daddy gave me lots of good ideas before I left for college. I short-sheeted my roommate's bed, put plastic wrap over the commodes, and rang all the room buzzers in the middle of the night, which got everyone out of bed at two in the morning. Amazing as it may sound, no one hated me. In fact, I started making friends—good friends. My roommate, Darlene, our friend Glenda, and I all sang three-part harmony a cappella. We actually stood up in the college cafeteria once and sang a nonsense song about a froggie being "a strange bird, who ain't got no tail, almost hardly ..." Our cafeteria audience threw money, and we got a standing ovation.

My journey with religion continued in college. I joined the Baptist Student Union. I even got a lead role in the live production of *Jesus Christ Superstar.* I was the hippie, the bad guy in conservative religion in those days. We did our performances in large churches all over Texas. I considered it flattering that a small part of the congregation would always get up and leave when I came singing down the aisle. That was when I began to question why there were people that my faith excluded.

Three wonderful girls lived down the hall from me in the dorm. They were stacked—huge breasts—they had bleach-white hair, and they wore tight clothes and short shorts. I noticed one day when I was out with my Baptist Student Union friends that they made fun of my three stacked friends, who looked different from us. I remembered the story from church when the woman was about to be stoned and Jesus said, "He who hath no sin cast the first stone." Who were we to judge these girls? I knew from dorm life with them that they were kind and considerate and always just as friendly as they could be. I saw exclusion more than I saw love and acceptance. That didn't feel Godlike to me. Also, the hell, fire, and brimstone sermons had made a huge impression on me. Maybe my insecurities drove that fear home harder than it did for most people. Was God fear, or was God love?

I was confused. I began to question my friendships, and then I began to question God. I prayed the oddest prayer: "God, please help me not be mad at you. Why do you and your followers exclude people? Why would you allow anyone to go to hell?"

About a week after I began praying this prayer, I was out on a city tennis court. I don't even play tennis, but that day I decided I should learn. There was no one else on the court, probably because it was really hot that day. I was standing there alone with a ball and a racket in my hand, and a handsome man about my age, twenty or so, joined me. He was dressed all in white—white Polo shirt, white tennis shorts, white shoes, and white socks. As he came toward me, the thought entered my mind that he was an angel. He asked if I played tennis, and I said no. Then he said it was awfully hot, did I want to just go sit under that tree over there and visit till it got a little cooler? We sat in the shade of the tree, and the stranger dressed in white changed my life.

I began pouring out my heart about being mad at God and people who excluded other people. His voice was so calm, his expression so pure. The first words he spoke were, "We are all one." The words took my breath away. He continued, "God loves us, all of us. There are no exceptions—all religions, all races, all people." He spoke words like this for around an hour. I just listened and soaked it all in like a balm. We never played tennis. I never saw him again.

The week after I met the beautiful man in white, I joined the Civil Rights Movement. I wore the clothes, grew my hair out long and straight, and marched for a cause I believed in all my life. I was always different. I grew up in a bigoted world, in the bigoted South, and in a bigoted family. I'm sure in lots of ways I was bigoted too, but I always knew it was wrong. One of the saddest experiences of my life involved a good friend of ours, a sixty-five-year-old black man named Raymond Monmoth.

On the railroad, Daddy was the conductor, and Raymond was the brakeman. While I was in college, Mama and Daddy began building a house.

They were doing all the work themselves, and Raymond, who also lived in Lufkin, came out regularly and helped. On one of the weekends I came in from college, Mama asked me to call Raymond and tell him I was home. He had asked to see me the next time I came in. I loved Raymond, but his dialect and demeanor made me sad. He never looked at me. His head was always bowed. When he talked, he always used phrases like, "Yezum, Mez Kang." When he was at our house and it was time to eat, Mama would always invite him in, but he would always refuse with profuse politeness and take his food on the steps of the back porch.

I made the phone call to Raymond, and a voice I didn't recognize answered the phone.

"Good afternoon, Monmoth residence." His diction was beautiful, elegant—that of a college professor.

I replied, "This is Linda King. May I speak to Raymond, please?"

"Oh, yezum, thank ya, Mez Kang. Thes be Ramen. How yu ben? I be mizzen ya."

I felt awful that this wonderful friend felt he had to pretend to be someone different around me. Raymond Monmoth was a pillar in his community. I later learned that he and his wife Lena took in countless kids, loved them like their own, paid for their educations, and sent them to college.

The Civil Rights Movement had to happen. How could we allow another generation of people to bow and scrape because of the color of their skin? "We are all one. God loves us, all of us. There are no exceptions—all religions, all races, all people."

By my senior year in college, I didn't like school any better. But, I liked myself more, and I had made lots of friends. My grades weren't great, but I graduated in three and a half years, receiving a Bachelor of Science degree with a major in Vocational Rehabilitation and Counseling. It was a new program at the time, and the whole concept made a lot of sense to me: the state was appropriating funds to train or retrain individuals who had special needs or handicaps and then place them in the workplace. Rehabilitation counselors were needed to facilitate the process.

After graduation, I was unable to find a job in the field of rehabilitation. So, in the spring of 1970 and at the "wise" age of twenty-one, I got a job with the Tuberculosis and Lung Association in Houston. I had never had a job before and was utterly unprepared for what I needed to do. I fumbled along there for about a year, feeling inadequate and insecure, and accomplished very little.

I decided that if I got married, all my problems would be solved. This was a mentality associated with the era in which I was born. Women were supposed to look for husbands and get married. I wasn't too keen on sex.

Actually, I thought I was a freak. I had no libido—one more deep, dark secret. I had graduated from college a virgin. I didn't know what was wrong with me, because I really liked men. I had boyfriends in college, and I enjoyed being with them. I just had no sex drive. But I had long since figured out that women could fake it, so I'd be all right.

Mama and Daddy loved each other and Denise and I, of that I was sure. They were my role models. I just knew I would be a great success at marriage and motherhood. My lifelong insecurities plagued me. I just wasn't cut out for the workplace. I decided I would find a husband and get married. That, I thought, would make me happy since marriage and family were good things.

Destiny led me to a good man. Bob was a Marine Corps lieutenant, was very handsome, had a college degree, and was very polite. Our fathers worked together, and our mothers were good friends who bowled together. Bob came home after a stint in Viet Nam, and our mothers introduced us at the bowling alley in Lufkin. We went out almost every night the week Bob was home. He was stationed in California, and I had my job in Houston. After several weeks of phone calls, Bob invited me to California. We decided to get married. We barely knew each other.

If the *Guinness Book of World Records* had a category for *Most Opposite Human Beings*, Bob and Linda could have made the record book. If I said black, he said white. For ten years we both tried very hard to be happy. We battled nonstop. Our differences were mental, physical, emotional, and spiritual. I rarely saw my parents fight in all my years growing up, but in this marriage of ours, we were in a constant state of disagreement. We seemed to have no common ground.

Twice I left him, only to return to try once again to reconcile a hopeless situation. I was of the mistaken opinion that it was not possible for me to get a divorce, and so we made each other miserable, never coming close to loving or caring about each other the way two people should. I knew from the beginning the marriage was wrong, but insecurities, fear, ego, and hardheadedness kept me stuck where I didn't belong. In the end, on my knees, sobbing, my last desperate attempt to make our marriage work, I begged Bob to just put his arms around me and hold me. It was something he had never been able to do. He couldn't hold me. Bob had endured a lot of pain in his life. We were both damaged. His cold hard simple answer, "No." made my final decision to leave.

Was it a wasted ten years? Absolutely not! We had two wonderful children and many hard-earned life lessons.

After ten years of unhappiness, I was thirty-two years old, leaving a miserable marriage in Socorro, New Mexico, with the only things that mattered to me: my eight-year-old son, Jace, and my four-year-old daughter, Tiffany. I felt completely worthless, as if no one in the history of time had failed as badly as I had. I was scared to death, and I had no job, two children to support, two hundred dollars to my name, and two little Pekingese dogs, Spot and Butch, which were the two things that mattered to Jace and Tiffany.

I was so afraid I wouldn't be able to support my children. Jace had a birth defect that affected the length of his left leg and foot. His left foot was deformed, with only four toes, measuring half the size of his right. What if Jace had special needs I couldn't afford? Tiffany was born with no abnormalities, but what if something happened to her and I was unable to find the money to cover her needs? Without the financial support I had inside my marriage, I was so afraid I would fail them. I couldn't eat or sleep because of my fear and the enormous guilt I felt for separating my kids from their father.

The day we packed up and I left Bob for the last time felt like death. As the kids and I pulled out of the dusty gravel driveway, through my rearview mirror I could see Bob crying as he stood on the porch waving good-bye. It all felt so incredibly sad to me that this man loved his wife and children, but found it impossible to show it. Bob's pain and the guilt I felt will be etched in my memory forever. Jace was riding in the front passenger seat, and tears were streaming down his cheeks. Tiffany, who was in the backseat looking back at her dad, innocently and confused, asked, "Mommy, why is Daddy crying?" I could not choke out an answer. My tears made it hard for me to drive. I began to pray silently. "Please, God don't let me let my babies down. Help me do this."

The day our little crew left Socorro, it was hot as Hades, and our little red Ford Fiesta had no air conditioning. We made it as far as Elephant Butte Reservoir, a small body of water desolate and devoid of anything living save a few lonely lizards. We were only an hour out of Socorro and still had thirty hours left to drive to my parents' home in Lufkin. It had to be at least 106 degrees outside. All four of my passengers were crying, moaning, sweating, and panting about the heat. So when I spied the reservoir, wet and inviting, I pulled the little red car off the road, drove right out through the desert, screeched to a halt, threw open my door, and screamed as loudly as I could, "Everyone in the water!" I didn't have to say it twice. The race was on: dogs, kids, and I dove, clothes and all, into the lukewarm water. It was heaven! Laughing loudly, arms outstretched toward the sky, coming up out of the water that day, I was born again, baptized with the knowledge that no matter what life had in store for me, no matter how many stinky-dog, hot-little-car, crying-children days I had ahead of me in this life, there would always be a lukewarm reservoir in which to fall, to cool my journey and help me on my way.

· · · · ·

LINDA'S LESSONS

Money is *not* the root of all evil! Insecurity is the root of all evil, and insecurity has played a very important role in my life. Insecurities rob your joy and squelch your chances for happiness. It is only when you decide that you are wonderful and love yourself that you can be of real value to your family, your friends, and this world. A man who believes in himself does not mentally or physically abuse his wife. A woman who knows her tremendous worth would never allow abuse. We guarantee our success in life through believing in ourselves and in our wonderful ability to affect the lives of others in a positive way.

Don't get married for the wrong reason. Please do not misunderstand. I believe in marriage, life partners, soul mates, love, and permanent unions, but only for the right reasons!

Destiny has a way of teaching us, if we are willing to learn. I used my first marriage as a way to avoid taking care of myself. My weakness caused a lot of pain for all parties involved. Although I don't believe in the kind of sin that leads to hell, fire, and brimstone, I do believe the worst thing we can do on this earth is hurt another human being. I also believe our karma will always be balanced and we will feel the pain we have caused, whether it is in this lifetime or another.

Lean on your Higher Power. Listen for guidance, and no matter how frightened you get, trust and do it! Staying in a counterproductive relationship due to fear or guilt is not only wrong for you, it is wrong for the person you are with. If you can't get out for yourself, do it for the other person. The negative energy that two unhappy people can produce affects all family life, especially children, and it even carries over into the workplace and throughout the universe. Our decisions—and the energy they produce—are like dominoes falling. Do the thing you know in your heart is right. Your soul always has the right answer.

I have such love and empathy for single parents. It is a really lonely and frightening place to be. If you are a single parent and going through fears of inadequacy and helplessness, call on your Higher Power. It works! It is as simple as saying out loud, "Help me!" And help is on the way. Throughout this book, you will read that I use this technique of asking for specific help over and over. I always, without fail, get my answer. You will too.

Oh, and never travel thirty hours in a really hot, little car with no air conditioning with two hot, crying children and two wet, hot, panting, stinky dogs. Did I mention Spot threw up three times before we crossed the New Mexico state line?

Chapter 3
The Lice Incident

My thirty-hour trip with two small kids and two small, wet dogs in a really hot little car smack in the middle of summer in the South had its challenges, but we made it home safely to Mama and Daddy.

My parent's place had a sprawling, manicured lawn; ancient, shady oak trees with Spanish moss dripping from the limbs; tall pines; elegant magnolias covered in white blossoms bigger than my hand; purple and yellow irises amongst lush ferns; banks of hot pink azaleas; a vegetable garden for as far as the eye could see, ending at the edge of a thick tangle of wild woods and underbrush; and a large, two-story house of multicolor brick with rough cedar trim that Mama and Daddy had finished with the help of many wonderful people, family, and friends. Kids, dogs, a carload of bags, and I were all welcomed with open arms and so much love. Jace, Tiffany, and I spent two years there while I went back to school to get a second degree in education. I'm proud to announce that this time around, I made straight As. I became an elementary school teacher. I am so appreciative of those years spent with my parents.

Beautiful portraits dance through my mind when I think back and see my two children in the garden with Daddy, or when I see Mama reading the kids' favorite stories to them. I tried to constantly let my parents know how grateful I was that they had provided a port in the storm and that they were such positive influences on my children. I'm still amazed at how graciously and lovingly they kept me and my motley crew. After all, I barreled in there with two kids, two dogs, and all the turmoil that goes along with an extra family moving on board.

Mama was an immaculate housekeeper, with pristine, white plush carpet, never a dish in the sink, and the laundry done every day without fail, even on Sunday. Daddy mowed and took care of the outside. The kids and I picked up after ourselves—no eating in the living room—and did our part where we could. I loved to cook and mother didn't, so I became the chef. We all got along amazingly well. Even the *lice incident* didn't shake them.

Yep, while I was doing my student teaching, I got a call one day that I needed to pick up Jace and Tiffany. They were in a different elementary school from the one in which I was working. I was horrified as the nurse calmly explained, "Ms. Cordell, both of your children are infested with head lice. You have to pick them up immediately, and they can't return to school until they have been treated and all nits have been removed to prevent them from spreading."

My ignorance of how lice were passed from one person to the next by simply jumping or flying caused me great embarrassment, as I was under the ignorant impression that lice were only associated with being dirty or staying in filthy living conditions.

After surviving the initial shock of the school nurse's call, I drove over to the kids' school. When I saw them, they were standing on the sidewalk with heads hung low. Jace had his arm over Tiffany's shoulder, trying to be the consoling big brother. She was crying and very embarrassed too. As they crawled into the car, Tiffany said through pitiful whimpering gasps of air, "Mama, Gammy is gonna kill us. We're in so much trouble."

"Gammy" and "Gop" were toddler Jace's recreation of Grandmamma and Grandpapa. As we pulled into the driveway, I said to the kids, "I'll walk into the house first. Y'all go straight up to your rooms, and I'll handle Gammy." Gammy the immaculate … oh, God!

As soon as we opened the door, heads tucked and fearful, Gammy and Gop jumped in front of us and started hopping up and down while scratching their heads, armpits, and butts. They then proceeded to sing, "Ooooohh ahhhh, lice! Darn little itchy, pesky, scratchy, egg-laying bugs in your head!"

Unbeknownst to Jace, Tiffany, and me, the school nurse had also called and informed Gammy and Gop that the kids had lice. Jace and Tiffany joined them doing the "lice dance," and we all laughed until we cried. Thank God for wonderful parents, especially those with a great sense of humor. That night, we all got shampooed with the special lice soap. For good measure, Jace got a really short haircut, and to avoid cutting Tiffany's long, blonde curls, Gammy and I stayed up all night picking nits out of her hair while Tiffany slept. I was determined the kids would not miss another day of school.

The whole lice adventure was a typical example of the great legacy of my mother and father. Laughter will make just about anything better. At the time the kids and I lived with my parents, none of us could know the huge challenges we would face in our future. Looking back, I now know it was learning to laugh even at the bad stuff that helped us through most of it.

I have always said about myself, "When I make mistakes, I make giant ones, but I do my damnedest not to make the same mistake again." I was determined that I would never have another relationship based on needing someone to take care of me. I worked hard in my education courses and at the same time took a correspondence course in interior design, which was something I loved to do. I was hired by the same school where I did my student teaching, and I began looking for a house to buy. I was going to be self-sufficient!

Jace, Tiffany, and I bought a small home in a tiny, one-red-light town called Huntington, only about ten miles from Gammy and Gop, and life was good. I was out on my own, taking care of myself and my children.

I adored my two kids, but being a single parent was a challenge. Each child handled the divorce in a different way. Tiffany was so young when Bob and I split up that she adjusted fairly easily. Jace was another story. He was angry and a handful. Sometimes my heart nearly broke as I watched his struggle. Sometimes I wanted to strangle him. The kids talked to Bob on the phone regularly, but they only got to see him once a year in the summer. I'd like to be able to say that I found the perfect solution for the behavior problems of a child hurt by divorce, but I can't. We took it one day at a time. Time seemed to help a little.

Two years following my divorce, I was a single mom trying my hardest to be a good parent on a limited income. In 1985, school teachers in East Texas qualified for food stamps, but I didn't care. I was too proud to accept assistance, and even though we didn't have any extras, we had a roof over our heads, enough food to eat, and each other. I derived such joy from knowing I was doing this on my own that I fully expected I would remain single forever, which just goes to show how wrong I could be … again!

· · · · ·

LINDA'S LESSONS

As a teacher, I adored every student, but the yellow birds were near and dear to my heart.

Never underestimate the importance of the role you play as a parent or grandparent. Please be aware of the energy you send out to children. If you have children, grandchildren, a relative's children, or only occasionally run across a child on an elevator or in a supermarket, be aware of the importance of your smile and your demeanor. Every second we spend on this earth loving, smiling at, hugging, speaking with, respecting, listening to, envisioning good things for, and believing in a child, we become cocreators in a wonderful human being and a better world.

Always be aware of the effect of your positive energy when around a child. As adults, it is our responsibility to surround any child—all children—with positive energy. It is my feeling there is nothing you could accomplish while on this earthly plane that could be more important than the impact you have on the children with whom you come in contact.

When I was a little girl, we had a family friend who I called Aunt Ruth. She was a precious older woman who had a talent for telling stories about little woodland animals who traveled on wonderful adventures. I adored the stories and couldn't wait to get to Aunt Ruth's house to scramble into her lap and listen, spellbound. Today, when I look into the bright blue eyes of my two grandchildren as they sit in my lap listening to stories of precious little woodland creatures, I understand the meaning of love that transcends time. Even if you only pass a child in a public place and make eye contact for a second, make that second count. Put on your brightest smile and send telepathic love and positive energy her way. It costs you nothing, but it may be a second she needs and remembers forever.

Positive energy cannot be expressed in a better way than laughter. We got head lice. We made it a party! Thanks, Gammy and Gop!

CHAPTER 4
ENTER: DON QUIXOTE

THANKS TO TOP RAMEN NOODLES AND pinto beans, I managed to scrape enough money together for Tiffany to take ballet lessons. While sitting in the "Mom waiting area," I met one of the other ballet moms, Tammye. She had a brother getting a divorce and knew for certain he and I would hit it off. I wasn't nearly so sure. But, in the early summer of 1985, I met Mike Thompson, a wild and crazy electrical contractor. He owned and operated a commercial and industrial electric company, which included wiring hotels and taking on large jobs for the state of Texas, doing highway work, wiring traffic signals and giant lights up and down the freeways. On the side, he bought and sold real estate.

Everything about Mike, including his personality, was electric. An angel he was not. He was a tad on the naughty side; he swore, drank, chased a lot of women, made a lot of money, and he made a few enemies because of it. But he was also brilliant, funny, and incredibly motivating. Mike stood about five foot six, a little on the short side for a man, but he was built like a bulldozer with broad, strong shoulders and tree trunks for legs. (I was the same height but really skinny.) He was hairy—not in a weird, back-hair, creepy way, but rather in a cute, cuddly-bear way. At thirty-five years old, his salt and pepper beard was more pepper than salt, and the constant grin that hid behind his whiskers was sexy and mischievous. His deep brown eyes were full of bullshit, but they had an intensity that made me weak in the knees.

On our first date, Mike asked me in his super thick East Texas accent (imagine a combination of Louisiana Cajun and John Wayne), "If you could be anything or do anything, and money was no object, what would it be?"

"I would buy and sell houses. I love to decorate," I said.

"I'll be damned. Real estate investin' is the thing I like to do most of all too. Why aren't you buyin' and sellin' houses?" he asked.

"Mike, I have about five dollars in my checking account right now. You obviously don't know how little school teachers get paid!"

He giggled and said, "You don't have to have money to do what you want to do."

Sarcastic but intrigued, I responded in a really lady-like way, "No shit?"

Then he proceeded to tell me the ins and outs of banking and how if you buy a house for eighty percent of its value or less, you don't need a down payment or possibly even closing costs. Next, Mike said something that was one of those golden moments in time, when you hear or read something that brands itself permanently in your brain: "Don't worry about the mule, just load the wagon."

He then told me if I found a house I wanted to buy, he would show me how to make money on it. Well, I couldn't help it. I was excited and began the search.

It was summer and I was off from school, so Mike popped by early one morning the week following our first date and our real estate discussion. He wanted me to put the house hunting on hold, leave the kids with my parents, and go to Dallas with him to help him bid on a bridge-straightening job for the state highway department. An eighteen-wheeler over the height restriction had driven under a bridge and dented the structure's metal beam. It would have to be heated with a red-hot rosebud torch and pushed back into place with a hydraulic jack Mike had specifically designed for the job.

I barely knew this man. I wasn't a prude, but I didn't normally run off to Dallas with strangers. I rationalized, "Mike isn't a stranger—after all, my daughter and his niece took ballet together. Besides, he's adorable, and I'm simply mesmerized." Everything about the man thrilled me. This job wasn't even an electrical gig, but he was taking it on because there was good money in it and he just knew he could do it. It seemed that all things were possible to him. Imagine—he wanted *me* to help him bid a job I knew absolutely nothing about! (Remember the little girl with all the insecurities.) Of course … I went.

As we drove to Dallas, he told me what equipment would have to be rented, how he paid his employees, how long the job would take, and how he usually figured his profit. Mike loved to gamble and loved to play games, so he proposed a little challenge.

He said, "I'm gonna figure the job and come up with a number to use as the bid, and you do the same. I want to see if you've been paying attention."

So, after looking at the site, plugging in all the numbers, and figuring a profit, I said smugly, "My bid is $12,400."

Mike grinned, nodded in approval, and announced, "I figured it and came up with $10,400. I'm going with your bid. You're gonna make me an extra two grand!"

I was shocked and horrified. If the bid was too high, he'd lose the job and it would be my fault. Sure enough, Mike turned my bid in to the state and got the job. He told me he knew from the first moment we met that I was brilliant; and then he took me to Cozumel, Mexico, on the extra $2,000.

Mike loved telling people how "easy" I was that I let him take me to Mexico on our first date. I have always staunchly held my ground that it was at least our third or fourth date!

Life was storybook-like. We were having so much fun. I had found a man who challenged my intellect and my emotions and treated me as his equal and his partner. I worried a little because Mike always had a large mug of rum and Coke in hand, but I never saw him drunk. Besides, he was spontaneous, kind, and generous, and he loved me.

Tiffany adored Mike. Jace, on the other hand, used to being the only man, wasn't impressed. He was still struggling emotionally, and like many preteens, he had a really bad attitude in general. Mike was like the pied piper though, and he worked at whittling away at Jace's resistance.

Mike had two beautiful daughters, Micah and Kresta, ages sixteen and twelve. The girls were reluctant, to say the least, to the idea of their dad's new girlfriend and her annoying "baggage." In the beginning, I think they wanted to murder Jace and Tiffany and vice versa, but eventually, as we all grew used to each other, acceptance slowly set in. Actually, Micah pretty much ignored us, as she had a whole other life full of boys and girlfriends, places to go, and things to do. Kresta, however, wound herself around my heart from the beginning. She was such a cute and funny child.

One of the first things I remember about Kresta is that she desperately wanted boobs. The first time Mike brought me to his home to meet Kresta, she asked me with eyes twinkling, "Linda, do you know how I can grow my boobs bigger?" She was only twelve. Was this a test?

"Well, sweetheart, I think your boobs are just fine the way they are."

"No, I want boobs like Dolly Parton!"

"You do?"

"Yep, and I've been askin' lots of people how to grow my boobs bigger, and they gave me some ideas. One lady said if I ate a whole loaf of bread every day my boobs would grow real big. Another woman told me if I put a mustard seed in my belly button, every day it was in there my boobs would grow bigger and bigger." With that said, Kresta lifted up her T-shirt to reveal a large piece of silver duct tape over her belly button. "It wouldn't stay in without the duct tape." In the next breath, she concluded, "And if the mustard seed doesn't work, I'm gettin' a boob job."

If it was a test, I failed because I couldn't top the mustard seed. I didn't try to discourage her in any way because I had a feeling that this child knew what she wanted, and someday she'd probably get it! I told her I was proud of her enthusiasm, and then we both giggled together about how flat chested I was too.

I couldn't believe I was seriously involved with someone, and even more unbelievable for me was that I had fallen in love. I can only remember Mike and I having one disagreement. I don't even recall why we argued, but I do remember how Mike apologized. I was teaching; in fact, I was at the chalkboard when there was a knock on the door and my principal, Mr. Cross, stuck his head in and asked to see me. There was a big smile on his face, so I knew not to be alarmed. Mr. Cross was holding a huge bushel basket of bright, shiny red apples. They were the biggest apples I had ever seen. There was a note on top that read, "If one apple will make a teacher happy, what will a bushel do?"

Our relationship grew stronger every day. Mike inspired me. He made me feel beautiful and brilliant. He put me on a pedestal, treating me like royalty while respecting me as his equal. Every day was filled with the unexpected, with love and with so much laughter.

Life, however, can change directions when you least expect it. Mike and I had been dating about six months when Micah was in a car accident. A young kid in a truck with huge monster tires briefly looked down to change the radio station, and by the time he looked up, he had rolled over the entire left side of the car next to him, a 1985 Mustang GT. Inside it was the sixteen-year-old daughter Mike worshiped. Micah sustained a serious brain stem injury and was in a coma. Life stopped. The fairy-tale romance was put on hold.

Weeks passed. Mike and I saw each other for short periods once or twice a week, but his whole life was now focused on his child who lay in a coma in a Houston hospital, fighting for life with every breath she took.

Three months passed before Micah opened her eyes and said, "Mom," to Rita, her mother. There was rejoicing, but we had no idea the long, hard road Micah had ahead of her. She awakened very slowly, and it became immediately obvious that Micah now had many handicaps. The blow to the back of her head affected her speech, swallowing, memory, and ability to walk; many of her intellectual skills were lost forever. Micah survived the car accident, but the vibrant teenager with her mother's beauty and Mike's charm was gone. Ignorance was our shelter, because looking back on that time, I remember we all thought she would have a full recovery.

Rita moved to Houston and got a job so she could be with Micah, who entered rehabilitation. Slowly, Micah relearned to eat, crawl, and eventually walk. The pain and suffering for Mike, Rita, and Kresta was indelibly stamped in their brains, as is the case with any loss, for the Micah they had known for sixteen years had vanished forever. Their grief was heavy, but as warriors do, they trudged along, facing each day one at a time.

Eventually life went on. Kresta, lonely and fearful, moved in with Mike and went back to school and friends. Rita stayed by Micah in Houston, watching with total anguish the rehabilitation process and struggles her daughter had to endure. Mike went back to work, visiting Micah on the weekends.

It had been six months since Micah's accident. Mike and I had been dating for a year. We were seeing each other daily except when he was out of town on a job or with Micah in Houston. Slowly, life began to have a semblance of normalcy. Mike was working full-time again and had a job in Freeport, Texas, installing one-hundred-foot light poles along the highway. I was teaching and nearing the end of another school year.

I started looking for a house to buy as an investment and found one. The asking price was $21,000. Good to his word, Mike showed me how buying it could be done. He told me to offer $11,000. With tongue in cheek, I made the offer. They took it! I was in shock, and now I had to get a loan. I went to four banks before I talked a banker into loaning me the money. I didn't sleep for a week. And on one of those sleepless nights, I got a phone call that changed my world.

It was May 15, 1986, around eleven o'clock at night. Jace and Tiffany were asleep. Mike was out of town on his job in Freeport, and I was in that tossing-and-turning mode when the phone rang.

Kresta, crying, almost whimpering, called to tell me her daddy had been in an accident. An oncoming car had rounded a curve in the wrong lane. To avoid a head-on collision, Mike had to swerve off the highway and landed in a deep ditch. When he tried to come out of the ditch, his truck flipped and he broke his neck. He was air-transported to Houston.

I got as many details as I could from Kresta and told her I was headed to the hospital, which was about a three-hour drive from Huntington. I soothed her as best I could, ended the call with her, and immediately called my close friend, Dale, who was a rehabilitation professor. I knew Dale could explain to me what a broken neck entailed. He told me it could be a situation where Mike would have to wear a neck brace until the neck set, if it was minor, or it could be as serious as total paralysis.

Kresta was in too much shock to travel to the hospital that night and stayed with friends. I loaded Jace and Tiffany up in our little vanilla Nissan Sentra, and we headed to Houston. As an eternal optimist, my thoughts while driving to the hospital that night were that Mike's injury would be minor. After all, how could two really bad things happen to one family within six months?

When I arrived at the emergency room, a young doctor wearing green scrubs entered the waiting area and sat down beside me. His expression was grave as he explained that Mike had severe trauma to cervical vertebrae four and five, which were located in his neck. He said he would like to show me the X-ray. I followed the doctor out of the waiting area, back toward the patient stations, and into a room with a lighted box displaying Mike's spine. The damaged vertebrae were obvious, even to me with no experience reading an X-ray, and the look on the doctor's face told the rest of the story.

His words pounded my head like a drum. "It doesn't look good," the young doctor whispered. "If he makes it through the night, we'll have to take it one day at a time. If he lives, he will probably be paralyzed from the neck down for the rest of his life."

· · · · ·

LINDA'S LESSONS

My favorite character in literature is Don Quixote, the Man of La Mancha. He was the dreamer of impossible dreams, the slayer of windmills. He fell in love with a barroom whore, Dulcinea. Don Quixote believed Dulcinea was a princess, and so she became one. Mike was my own personal Don Quixote. He believed anything was possible. I became the best I could be because he believed in me. Believing in and showing love to those you should love the most can turn weakness into power, insecurities into confidence, and fear into bravery. Mike believed in me more than I believed in myself, and it was Mike's unwavering confidence in me, "the yellow bird," that gave me wings to fly.

Chapter 5
"A Little Minor Setback"

"Paralyzed from the neck down for the rest of his life." I don't think I responded to that young ER doc. I remember the tears welling up in my eyes. I was frozen in place, and I believe the doctor put his hands on my arms and turned me around to head me back toward the waiting area. His voice was barely audible as he said, "I'm sorry."

As we walked out of the X-ray room, I saw a gurney coming out of one of the draped enclosures. It was Mike. His head was slightly elevated and his body completely draped in a white sheet. The doctor told me they were taking him to the Intensive Care Unit (ICU). Mike opened his eyes. He saw me, smiled, and stuck his tongue out at me. I began to laugh and cry. I managed to say, "I'm here, babe," as his so-still body disappeared into an elevator.

Denise was living in Houston at the time, and she picked up Jace and Tiffany so they could stay with her while I spent the remainder of the night sleeping off and on in the ICU waiting area. This night was a major turning point in my life. During my fitful sleep, my wonderful grandmother came to me from the other side. Granny stood there, just watching me and looking at me peacefully while her body emitted a heavenly white light. Her face had a beautiful, serene expression, and without words she communicated to me that everything would be okay and that I was making the right decision to stand by Mike.

That long night in ICU, with sleep a hit and miss, the age-old question of destiny verses choice floated in and out of my thoughts. As my heavenly ghost dissipated, the answer came to me with perfect clarity: It's not destiny or choice. It's both. Our lives have a definite path, thus destiny, but at important junctures, we must make a choice. I had two children to think about. They came first for me, but I loved Mike. They needed me. Mike needed me. I had to make a choice.

I weighed the decision back and forth, back and forth. I thought about my parents and the time Jace, Tiffany, and I were driving to Lufkin, coming home for a visit. Bob and I had moved to Wyoming. Tiffany was only two years old. She got sick—really sick. I had to stop and take her to the hospital in Denver, and she was diagnosed with spinal meningitis. One call to Mama, and she instantly replied, "I'll call the station and tell them to get Daddy off the train in Nacogdoches. We're on our way, sweetie. We'll be there, baby, hold on."

It was a rough two weeks in the Denver Children's Hospital, but Tiffany miraculously came out fine. "We'll be there, baby, hold on."

That's who we were. We were people who were there for the ones we loved. I learned that from my parents, and Jace and Tiffany would learn that from me. My decision was made. I chose Mike and my children.

At around seven o'clock the following morning, I was awakened by the neurosurgeon assigned to Mike. He introduced himself, and I explained to the doctor that Mike and I were not married, but I was there to stay as long as Mike needed me. After all these years, I still find it hard to believe what the doctor said next.

"The worst thing about an injury like this is that he can't even use his hands to pick up a gun and blow his brains out."

I was speechless at first and outraged beyond measure, but I ignored the doctor's appalling words and began to ask questions about Mike's current condition—his vitals, if he was stable. The physician answered each question with reproach, treating me as if I had little or no brain. Shortly after the neurosurgeon took his leave, the hospital offices opened. I marched into the department of neurosurgery and demanded a new doctor. Unfortunately, the new doctor could not change the outcome. Mike's paralysis was permanent.

That same morning, I called Mr. Cross, my principal, and told him about Mike's accident. Since there were only two weeks left in the school year, I told him that I would get out the report cards from the hospital if he would get a substitute for me. I was not going to leave Mike, and he understood completely. Mr. Cross was one of the most spiritual beings I had ever met, so I asked him to pray with me.

This big, beautiful man with a voice larger than life spoke God's language. We prayed together on the phone that morning. He was one of the many earthly angels sent to me. As Mr. Cross prayed, his deep, resonating voice soothed my soul, and at the same time, I felt the arms of our Source enfold me.

My job was no longer an issue. Denise, Mama, Daddy, and Tammye, Mike's sister, took care of Jace and Tiffany. The vigil began. For the next two weeks, I lived in the ICU waiting lounge, only leaving long enough to take a quick shower every few days at Denise's house. The first week, Mike drifted in and out of consciousness. I could only see him four times a day for about fifteen minutes each visit. Some of the time he was hallucinating, but I think he always knew when I came in the room.

Often when I entered for my scheduled visit, Mike would be seeing monsters and devil-like figures. It was horrifying, and I could do nothing to ease his fears. Mostly his attempts at speech were futile; he made no sense. He was on so much medicine to sedate him and to fight infection. He felt no pain. Ironically, this was an unfortunate development, as the doctor explained to me. When they tested for sensation throughout Mike's body, Mike could neither move nor feel anything from his toes to his shoulders. His vitals did, however, continue to improve daily, and after the tenth day the doctor reported Mike was no longer critical.

It was at that point I walked into Mike's ICU stall. His eyes were bright, he had a huge smile on his face, and what he said was the most astonishing thing I had ever heard.

His words flooded out, "Hey, babe, how long have I been in here? I have a job to get finished. I was supposed to be in Bill's office at the state highway department on the sixteenth. Could you call him for me and tell him I've had a little minor setback? Does anyone know where my diary is? It was in my truck when all this happened."

I swear, God as my witness, Mike called his accident a "little minor setback." Mike's "diary" (what most people call a "day-timer") was his Bible. It contained every telephone number, every job number, and every tiny bit of information he didn't want to commit to memory, even though his memory was phenomenal. I instinctively knew Mike didn't want or need to hear a bunch of crap about how he didn't need to worry, or for him to forget work. I knew he needed me to fly into action, and I did.

The next words out of my mouth were, "I'll handle anything you need." At that moment, I became Mike Thompson's arms and legs.

For the next few days, I conducted business for him on the payphone in the ICU waiting room (cell phones were not a luxury we had at the time). I found his crushed truck, only a short drive from Houston, and within it, the much-coveted diary. We were in business. I took notes and called Mike's secretary in Lufkin with his instructions. We were actually running a company out of the ICU. Within a few days, Mike was moved into a private room. We made a list of everything he would need to run his business from the hospital room and called his foreman, Leonard, to come up and talk with him. It was a Saturday. I propped Mike up in bed, washed his face, brushed his teeth, carefully covered him with a sheet, and made him ready for Leonard's visit.

Leonard, a friend of Mike's for many years, entered the room, head bowed and eyes glistening with tears. It was the first time he had seen Mike since the accident. He could barely get out, "Hello, Mike."

Mike helped with a voice as bright as if they were in a bar sharing a beer, which they had done on several occasions, to say the least. "Hey, Leonard, we have a job to finish. Linda's the boss now, and anything she tells you and the guys to do, get it done!"

Mike continued to list everything he expected Leonard to accomplish in the following week, and Leonard started smiling from ear to ear and said, "Okay, Mike. We'll do it."

There had to be a least a million guardian angels surrounding me at the time because I didn't question his words any more than Leonard did. Each night when Leonard called, I relayed Mike's instructions for the following day.

The first week we were in a private room, Mike's neurosurgeon came in carrying a large metal apparatus called a halo brace. The doctor looked at me and asked, "Do you have weak stomach, or can you help? The nurse is busy."

He needed to literally screw stainless steel bolts into Mike's head to straighten and hold his spine in place. I don't have a weak stomach, so I held Mike's head and assisted while the doctor deadened Mike's scalp in four places and then screwed all four bolts into his skull and attached the metal halo. When it was in place, it formed a complete circle that sat above his head like an angel's halo, which was quite ironic because, as I said earlier, Mike was not an angel. Metal arms came down from the circle that attached to a thick plastic, fleece-lined vest. Mike looked like a cross between Frankenstein and Madonna without the cones. He took it in perfect stride, and like we reacted to everything else that was wild and strange in our new world, we laughed.

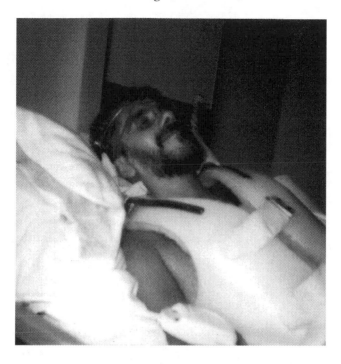

My children were amazing through all of this. On the weekends, they would bring pallets and pillows and spend the nights with us. Jace was an entrepreneur. I didn't know it at the time, but at age eleven, he would leave the room, supposedly on a mission to get food, but what he was actually doing was charging people to ride the hospital elevators. He later confessed he made five dollars or more on each "mission," charging a quarter a person. Sometimes he took his seven-year-old sister, and together, they sneaked into the surgery observatory rooms and watched live surgeries. I suppose the lesson to learn here is no matter how bad things get, it's still possible to have a great time, learn something new, and make a little money on the side.

Kresta, now thirteen and not to be outdone by the two little kids, came up to the hospital one weekend to take care of Mike for me while I went home to Huntington on business. She brought her best friend Angie. While they watched movies on the VCR Mike had me install in the hospital room, the girls painted Mike's toenails fuchsia, purple, and candy apple red. The best part was the look on the faces of the nurses and aides as they tended to Mike and discovered his newly painted toenails for the first time! Mike would always respond with a huge smile, and with pride he'd say, "They're *great*, aren't they?"

• • • • •

LINDA'S LESSONS

Sometimes life just stinks. Become bitter and give up? Never. Mike had a choice. His plight was as horrific as they come. He could have given up and been mad at the world and taken it out on everyone in it. No one would have blamed him. His oldest daughter had just been in a catastrophic accident, and although Micah's life was spared, the daughter he had raised was gone forever. As if the pain of losing a daughter was not bad enough, Mike was faced with battling for his own life, and he could have chosen defeat. Instead, he chose to be positive, to believe in a cure for paralysis, and to appreciate the people who stood by him. He loved me beyond limits and even went a step beyond by becoming my teacher. In the years to come, Mike's "little minor setback" would also teach countless other people the art of handling the worst of situations with dignity, grace, humor, and wisdom beyond measure.

Chapter 6

A Promise

By the end of the summer, we were still in the hospital with no end in sight because Mike had gotten a pressure wound, also known as a bed sore. These are horrific, tunneling wounds that are only visible after all the damage is done. First, you notice a small opening in the skin, but by that time the rotting flesh underneath the skin could be as large as your fist or bigger. These wounds often happen to victims of paralysis because they cannot feel the pain that would usually trigger a person to shift positions and take the pressure off that particular spot.

Mike's first pressure wound, involving his entire lower back, was so bad a surgeon had to carve a twelve-inch diameter flap of skin, lay it open, scrape out all the dead tissue and leave it open and exposed to the air to begin to heal. About a week later, the doctor took Mike back to surgery and closed the wound. A week after that, when I turned Mike over to bathe his back, the odor coming from the wound just about knocked me over. The nurse peeled back the bandage, and we saw the wound was oozing a ghastly gray-colored juice that smelled more putrid than anything I could have ever imagined. The surgeon had to start all over—and that is how a pressure ulcer kept us in the hospital for an extra three months.

Due to Mike's pressure wound, he was issued a Clinitron Bed. It was a giant sandbox with an amazing liner covering the sand. The liner kept the sand off the skin but allowed air that was continually moving the sand to blow through to Mike's body. The constantly moving sand shifted the pressure 24/7. In my opinion, a quadriplegic should never be on any other kind of bed. This Clinitron Bed was so huge that Mike and I slept together in it every night. The nurses and aides had all gotten used to these two crazy people who ran an electrical contracting business from a hospital room, slept together in the hospital bed/sandbox, and basically acted as if they were in the Hilton instead of the hospital.

It was the end of August, and school would start again soon. I didn't want to leave Mike. I knew he didn't want me to go back to school, but I'm sure he had no idea how to ask me to take on such a big responsibility for a lifetime. There was also the issue of sexuality. In Mike's mind, I'm sure it was inconceivable that I would be willing to forgo that part of my life due to his handicap. What he didn't know—my dark little secret—was that I wasn't a sexual being. I loved from the depth of my soul, but sexually, I faked it because I had no libido. It still amazes me to think about the perfect details of my life that allowed me to take this path.

I took matters into my own hands. I climbed in bed with Mike, and he began telling me how much he appreciated me and loved me, as was the case every night. I told him I didn't want to leave him to go back to teaching and that I was committed to anything and everything we would have to face together as long as he wouldn't change. I told him that I expected him to continue to be the funny, precious, brilliant, loving guy I had come to love over the past sixteen months. And Mike, cocky, always cocky, asked me if I would change. He said he expected me to continue to be the sexy, brilliant, funny, happy, and enthusiastic person he had come to love.

We both promised we wouldn't change, and then I said, "Mike, will you marry me?" For the first time since the accident, Mike cried. He couldn't move anything but his head, so I picked up his arms, put them around me the best I could, and kissed his tears away.

He whispered, "Yes."

• • • • •

LINDA'S LESSONS

Sweet irony. I left a man who could have held me but wouldn't, and I married a man who would have held me but couldn't.

We promised we would never change. We were both so wrong! We would both change by leaps and bounds. Over the next eighteen years, we made each other better. We both had so much to learn from one other, which was, of course, the reason for our journey together. Mike tended to make money his first priority in life and wasn't afraid of anything. I put people first and was afraid of everything. Mike taught me to, as he said over and over, "Walk in like you own the place." I taught him that how he treated people would be his most important life accomplishment.

CHAPTER 7
TOUCH A SPOT

IT IS MY BELIEF THAT BEFORE coming to earth, we plan our journey, which is the reason I had gotten my first degree in Rehabilitation Counseling. Although I didn't use my degree for thirteen years after I graduated from college, the information was neatly tucked away and readily available when it came time for Mike to leave the hospital. Because of a lifetime of speeding tickets (remember that whole bad-boy syndrome), Mike had no car insurance. Even worse, his health insurance had lapsed the month before.

His hospital bill was enormous. He also had no funding for the important process of rehabilitation, which would teach him how to live with his all-encompassing handicap. The day we received the bill in the hospital was frightening. I had been helping Mike handle Micah's insurance and knew her policy was about to limit out. Two catastrophic accidents six months apart; what a mess we were in.

Mike was calm, unafraid, and intense. Looking directly into my eyes, he began, "Linda, I need you to call the hospital operator and ask to speak to the CEO. Tell him about Micah's accident, that she had insurance but the policy is about to limit out. Then tell him I have no insurance. You are our best shot, Linda. He will be more sympathetic with it coming from a woman."

I picked up the phone and made the call. To my amazement, the operator put me through. The man I spoke with was surprisingly kind. He listened to every word and then, without hesitation, he said, "Your bill is taken care of."

I began to cry, and then I thanked him profusely. It felt like I could hear him smiling. What a wonderful person. We had encountered another angel. Mike was smiling, with tears in his eyes. I hung up the phone, and Mike said with pride, "I didn't have a doubt you could do it."

Next, I made a few calls, and Texas Rehabilitation Commission (TRC, today known as the Department of Assistive Rehabilitative Services) picked up Mike's case. TRC sent him to a rehabilitation facility near the hospital so that he could begin the arduous task of learning how to exist in his new world without the ability to move or feel except with his head and shoulders. The first major hurdle was to simply get used to sitting up without his blood pressure going haywire. It took days, but once Mike's blood pressure stabilized in a sitting position, the occupational therapist taught him how to operate a power wheelchair using an elaborate mouthpiece attached to the chair and a sipping and puffing action. I was taught the fine points of using a manual chair and how to transfer Mike in and out of it, the power chair, and the shower chair … lots of chairs became a part of our new world.

We had to learn what a "bowel program" was. Since the paralysis had affected Mike's insides as well as the outside of his body, it was necessary to facilitate his bowel movements with scheduled stool softeners and laxatives and a process done with a gloved finger called "digital stimulation." I also had to learn to catheterize him to relieve his bladder, in addition to countless other "medical pleasantries" most typical fiancées do not encounter. We had entered the twilight zone.

I will never forget the day the nurse came in to teach me how to catheterize Mike. I smiled sweetly at Mike and the nurse and proclaimed, "Hey, babe, you taught me to operate your backhoe and crane, how hard can this be?"

Instantly Mike, not feeling nearly so eager, reminded me that *this* was not a backhoe or a crane! The catheterization process had to be done every four hours.

I also had to learn how to conduct Mike's physical therapy and range of motion exercises. The physical therapist taught me how to transfer Mike into and out of bed and into and out of the car. In the beginning, our only form of transportation was my little Nissan Sentra, a tiny two-door car with bucket seats. With neither of us gainfully employed, a new, handicap-equipped van was not an option at this time. Lifting Mike was like picking up a 160-pound sack of potatoes. At the time, I was a whopping five-foot, six-inch, 118-pound fireball. Nothing could stop me! The first time I tried to transfer Mike out of the car, it took me forty-five minutes. Eventually, I could transfer Mike into the car, raise the bucket seat into an upright position, strap him in, throw the manual wheelchair into the trunk, and be in the driver's seat in less than three minutes.

Often, people who didn't know any better referred to Mike as *paraplegic* because it was the only term they knew. A paraplegic has an injury low enough on the spine that their arms and hands are not affected. Mike was *quadriplegic* because all four limbs were paralyzed. Mike had to be fed, bathed, dressed, teeth brushed, and nose hairs removed. He could no longer do anything for himself, except think and talk. He was brilliant, and so he did a lot of both. But, wow, we had so much to learn, and we did.

After about three weeks into our stay in the rehab facility, Mike had gotten the hang of operating the power wheelchair with the sip-and-puff apparatus that he used with his mouth. He was able to move himself from point A to point B for the first time in four months—since his accident.

We called in the staff chaplain, and on September 28, 1986, Mike and I were married during a private ceremony in the garden of the rehabilitation center. Mike wore a white cotton sweat suit because zippers, or anything that could cause pressure wounds, were strictly forbidden. My outfit matched perfectly. I wore a pink sweat suit with a pink and white flower garland in my hair. We cried, laughed, and kissed through the entire ceremony. Two incredible optimists joined mind, body, and soul, neither one knowing how hard and how wonderful their union would be.

Mike was supposed to stay in rehab for six months, but after the first month, he called the doctor into his room and said in his thick East Texas accent, "There's not a whole hell of a lot more y'all are going to be able to teach me or Linda, and I'm ready for you to sign me outta here."

The doctor was surprised to say the least. Mike continued, "I'd be a whole lot more comfortable sitting at home on my back porch looking at my eighty-five acres and my pond than being cooped up in this place. I really do thank y'all for everything you've showed us, but we're leaving." Mike wouldn't take no for an answer. The doctor signed the order, and we were out of there.

The trip home was rather somber until we reached a mall about an hour from home. Mike insisted I stop and run in without him to get some essentials we would need once we got to the house. He told me to park in the handicap spot next to the door, roll down the windows, and he would be fine. I was terrified at the thought of leaving him alone, but one thing that certainly had not changed since Mike's accident—and never did change—he wasn't afraid of anything, and he would always make his wishes known. It was fall, the weather was cool, and I would only be gone about ten minutes, so I agreed. I flew into the store, gathered only necessities, and raced back outside, panting, only to see Mike sitting there with a huge grin on his face. I jumped into the car and asked what was so funny.

Mike giggled and said, "A policeman stopped by and poked his head through the window and told me I'd have to move the car because we're in a handicap parking space with no handicap sticker. I told him I was handicapped but just didn't have my sticker yet. He didn't believe me. So then he asked me where was I handicapped, and I told him … *Touch a spot.*"

From that day forward, when things were going really badly or we happened to be feeling down, our pat explanation to the question, "What is wrong?" was always, "Touch a spot."

· · · · ·

LINDA'S LESSONS

For the next eighteen years, no matter how bad things got, through bladder infections, pressure wounds, and hospital stays, Mike never once took out his anger, frustration, or sadness on me. Instead, when things got really bad, we cried together and then usually found a way to laugh. Mike Thompson: my hero.

I am often asked how I made the decision to marry Mike after his accident, knowing the extent of his injury and disabilities. The answer isn't simple. The most obvious reason to anyone who knew Mike was that he was an incredible person, brilliant, funny, and optimistic! Probably the easiest answer to understand is that I loved him. I also didn't know any better. I had no way of knowing how difficult it would be. The complex answer, the reality of which I am now sure, is that marrying Mike was my destiny. I had guidance from the other side. Seeing my grandmother in that vivid dream left no doubt that standing by Mike was the right decision. Please understand, I am not special in any way. The gift of receiving spiritual guidance is not exclusive to a few of us. Instead, it is available to all! The trick is asking for and believing in your gift when it arrives.

Chapter 8
The Miami Project

Mike and I drove the rest of the way to Huntington discussing our future. We decided to sell my little house and move into Mike's four-bedroom brick home. Then, Mike confided that he felt he could no longer stay in the electrical business since he couldn't strap on his tools and get in the trenches with his crew. He also told me that he had close to a half million dollars in business debt, which would have to be repaid because whatever we ended up doing, we had to take care of our bankers. I was hanging on every word and to this day still do not know why I wasn't terrified. Mike, the motivator ...

We were optimistic about our challenges and the future. Our saving grace was that Mike's shop and all of the electrical equipment inside was paid off, free and clear. He owned cranes, backhoes, a bulldozer, a trencher, and a huge warehouse full of electrical supplies. We went right to work, held an auction, and sold almost everything to the highest bidder. The auction paid off 75 percent of the bank loans, and the remainder was set up on a monthly note. Mike kept three large pieces of equipment out of the auction, spread the word to fellow electrical contractors that the equipment was for rent, and we had an income. Mike, always ready to rock and roll, even from a wheelchair, had a lot more in mind.

Real estate investing was one of Mike's real talents. Aside from the electrical business, Mike owned several rental houses. He had already built three duplex apartments and loved flipping fixer-uppers. One evening a couple of weeks following the auction, Mike and I were sitting on the back porch of his sprawling ranch-style home.

Mike asked, "Hey, babe, you told me when we first met that if you could do anything in the world, you'd buy and sell houses. How 'bout we go find the cure for paralysis and then we make buyin' and sellin' real estate our full-time job?"

My response was an affirmative, "I'm hooked. You showed me I could do it once. Let's do it again!"

The week before Mike's accident, I had found a local banker, Mark, to loan me the money for the little house I had found to buy. Mike was right. I didn't have to have a penny. The loan included enough money to fund the house and the closing costs. With Huntington having a population of less than two thousand counting cats and dogs, word of Mike's accident spread rapidly. The third day after Mike was in intensive care, I got a call at the hospital from the bank.

Mark was wonderful. He told me he knew what had happened to Mike, and that if I wanted to back out he would get my earnest money refunded without a problem. I told him I needed a day to think about it. Before going to sleep that night, I prayed for an answer. When I woke up, I knew Mike would be disappointed in me if I didn't go through with the deal. I called Mark and told him I was going to call the realtor who had listed the house. If I could get her to drive to Houston with the closing documents and a contract to put the house back on the market immediately, I would go for it.

My realtor did not hesitate. She made the three-hour trip to Houston. I signed all the paperwork. The realtor never even moved her sign. Two weeks later, I sold the house for a four-thousand-dollar profit, and I never even made the first payment. Four thousand dollars to a school teacher existing on wages qualifying for food stamps was like winning the lottery! I was hooked on buying and selling real estate! This experience had a lasting effect upon my life, essentially opening my eyes to financial possibilities I had never considered. Little did I know it was also a foreshadowing of things to come.

The back porch would become one of Mike's and my favorite places to brainstorm, dream, and plan for the future. Financially, we had a plan. How we would survive parenthood and raising our four kids was up in the air.

By this time, Micah had also completed her rehabilitation and had returned home to live with Rita in Huntington. Through intensive rehab, she regained the ability to walk with a slight gait problem. Her right hand was permanently curled and unusable. Micah's speech was severely impacted, and after numerous attempts to repair her vocal cords, her voice was raspy and whisper-like. Only those of us who were family and with her often could understand her attempts at conversation. Micah's mental capabilities were diminished to that of about a twelve-year-old, and most of her reading and math skills were lost forever.

With the grace and tenacity that mimicked her father's, Micah got a job at a local grocery store. Each day, she walked to work, where she dusted, stocked shelves, and sacked groceries. Huntington High School awarded her an honorary high school diploma, and she walked across the stage with her graduating class in May of 1987.

Jace resented Mike, me, and everything in his whole world. He pouted and was belligerent, regardless of Mike's and my attempts to make him happy. One afternoon, I found him down in the shop, which was practically empty because of the auction. Mike had not sold some of his communications equipment because he could get a better price elsewhere. When I walked in the shop, Jace was in an open loft tossing hundreds of dollars' worth of phones over the side and watching them burst into pieces when they hit the concrete floor. I was horrified and furious. At age twelve, Jace towered over me by almost six inches and outweighed me by sixty pounds. I grabbed a set of jumper cables from the shop floor and chased him for ten minutes, with the intent to beat him to within an inch of his life. Thank God I didn't catch him. I wanted to murder him.

Grounding Jace didn't work. He would sneak out. Mike offered to pay him to do jobs we needed, but Jace wouldn't work. He wouldn't get out of bed in time to catch the bus. Every morning was a shouting match. On one such occasion, I almost lost my mind. Jace, purposefully sauntering at a snail's pace to the door, turned around to me and shouted, "Take me to school! I missed the bus!"

I know I shouldn't have, but I got right in his face and snarled, "Today you'll walk."

He drew back his fist. Silence. We stared. Slowly he lowered his arm, but through gritted teeth, he spat out what he knew would break my heart: "I want to move to Dad's."

I surprised him by walking straight to the phone and calling Bob. Bob and I were much better friends divorced than we had been married. He and I had already discussed Jace's attitude.

I began, "Bob, Jace missed the bus again today. He just drew back his fist to hit me and he wants to come live with you."

"Send him on," was Bob's ex-Marine Corp lieutenant reply. Bob was lean and mean. He ran marathons and lifted weights daily. My "precious" son had been living on easy street, and all that was about to change.

The next day, I put Jace on a plane to his dad's. I could tell he kept expecting me to cry, knowing what a softy I was. This man-child had just threatened to hit me. I shed no tears. A week after Jace left, I got a call from Bob while Jace was in school.

"Our young man had to have an attitude adjustment two days ago. I told him when he arrived he would do his homework every night before he ate supper, which he would cook every other night. He would join the basketball team. He would also have to keep his room clean, do his own laundry, wash dishes every night, and help me clean the whole house every weekend, and after he took a shower he was to clean up the bathroom and take a towel and dry the shower inside and out. I gave him a couple of days to adjust, and then on the third night, when he didn't dry the shower, I went in and asked him why he didn't dry the shower. He informed me it was stupid. I forcefully explained to him that it didn't matter how stupid he thought it was—this is my house and he would do everything I told him to do, including wiping down the shower. Jace drew back his fist. I shoved both my hands into the young gentleman's armpits, lifted him off the floor, and slammed him into the bathroom wall. His feet didn't touch the ground. Then I carefully explained, 'Jace, when you swing, you better give it all you've got, and you better knock me out, because if you don't, I will send you home to your mother in a box!' The shower has been dry every night since."

Jace stayed with Bob for the next couple of years, and I was so thankful for the wonderful things he was able to accomplish with our son. Jace learned to play basketball and dropped forty pounds. He looked great, did really well in school, and even got the lead role in his school play. The best part was that even though he was thousands of miles away from me, Bob helped me get my son back. Jace and I spoke on the phone once or twice a week. I could hear the progress he was making in his voice. We saw each other every six months, and he stayed with us during the summer. Several times, Jace asked if he could move home with Mike and me. It was really hard for me to say no, but Bob and I agreed; Jace had made this decision, and now he would have to live with it. One year became two, and Jace was turning into a wonderful young man. His anger turned into humor—what a delightful change.

Jace and Micah had a special bond that was forged in heaven. Micah, unlike Mike, didn't have quite the same positive attitude about her situation and often got depressed. Jace could snap her out of it. During the first summer visit after he moved in with his dad, Jace realized Micah was in a particularly foul mood. He took it upon himself to make her laugh.

Now, most teenage stepbrothers in this kind of situation might put their arm around their disabled, depressed stepsister and say encouraging words like, "It will be okay," or "Life sucks, but you've got to stay positive." That wasn't Jace's method. Instead, he sat with her on the floor, meditated, and channeled the spirit of the "Great Babarama."

One of the only sounds Micah made really well was the "Ommm" sound, commonly used in mediation. Knowing this, Jace had her close her eyes and hum "Ommm." As soon as Micah started trying to "Ommm," all thoughts of depression vanished, and she began to laugh. Jace then feigned sternness and insisted that Micah be serious, which caused more attempts of "Ommm" and more laughter. Jace fabricated a wild story of a past life where he was the Great Babarama and she was Shena, the warrior princess.

After they both took their mediation stances, Jace chanted mantras like, "Oh, Shena, strong and vibrant warrior princess, I, the Great Babarama, am here to bring you great positive energy. You will not have a shitty attitude anymore (Micah laughs). You will not be depressed or be a pain in the ass (Micah doubles over in laughter). You are now in a world that is happy and full of much love, sex, laughter, and men with giant penises (Micah falling backward and laying full out onto the floor laughing). All you have to do is say 'Ommm' in order to be transformed into this wonderful life where men adore and worship you."

There was no way Micah could "Ommm" at this point because she was laughing too hard, but it didn't matter because her shitty attitude was indeed forgotten until the next occasion when the Great Babarama was needed to bring her out of her funk.

One Christmas, years after the Great Babarama and Shena were staples in our life; the entire family picked up Jace at the airport. This was still at a time pre-9/11, and we all were allowed to wait for Jace at the gate. Kresta had the genius idea for us to drape multicolored sheets around our shoulders and heads, mimicking the hijab's worn by Muslim women and/or outfits adorned by Hare Krishnas.

Mike in his wheelchair, both my parents, Kresta, Tiffany, and I, with Micah standing out in front, all adorned with bed sheets over our heads, began to chant "Ommm, oh, Great Babarama, welcome home. We worship you!" as Jace walked off the plane. We even had a sign that read, "WELCOME HOME GREAT BABARAMA." Was the entire display offensive to anyone of the Muslim faith? Yes, horribly but not intentionally, and I'm sure it really perturbed any Hare Krishna onlookers as well. Should we have been arrested? Yes, we should have been, especially when I look back on it and think about what would have happened to us had we pulled the stunt in 2010. Were we arrested? No. Did we embarrass the hell out of Jace? Yes, and it was probably the only time in his life that we succeeded in embarrassing him. The entire gate of people, crowded and waiting to greet their loved ones, were laughing over this freakish, insane family, who were not religious zealots but simply wanted to play a practical joke.

Aside from all the practical jokes, our life in Huntington, away from the hospitals and rehab facilities, included the normal stuff—school, work managing the equipment rentals, taking care of a household—and the not-so-normal stuff too. Every day was a struggle keeping Mike off his butt long enough to avoid pressure wounds. He hated being in bed, but he couldn't feel the pain from sitting in his wheelchair too long in one position. I became his personal monitor, forcing him to lie down from time to time, which he hated.

Mike was hell-bent on making sure the rental business and all our finances were worked out while I researched a cure for paralysis and took care of the family and him. My search led me to information on the Miami Project, which was the world's largest research center dedicated to finding a cure for paralysis. It was located in Miami. Mike, always proactive, decided the only way for us to really find out about the program was to fly to Florida. Getting a quadriplegic on an airplane is a trick but doable, and so we did it.

Mike didn't have a negative bone in his body. He taught me that all things are possible. One of his favorite expressions when I was a little afraid of trying something new was, "Walk in like you own the place." I learned to ask for help wherever we went, and we needed a lot of it! People were always more than happy to lend a hand. Thus, with the help of many wonderful employees working for the airlines, a twelve-inch-wide aisle chair, and the patience of a planeload of passengers, we boarded a 747 flight to Miami.

Once at the Miami Project headquarters, we discovered the many research programs, treatment possibilities, and innovative surgeries the program offered. Biofeedback, functional electrical stimulation, and aggressive physical therapy were options that might benefit Mike, so we decided to find a way to get weekly treatments. I called the airlines and asked for their help. I told our story and expressed our needs. For the next twelve weeks, Mike and I flew first class for a fare of fifty dollars each round trip from Houston to Miami.

Once a week for those twelve weeks, Mike and I would get up at two o'clock in the morning and drive the two-and-a-half-hour trip from Huntington to Houston's airport. We would fly to Florida, travel by rental car to two or three different types of therapy or doctor appointments, and be back on the flight home by six o'clock the same night. We would arrive back in Huntington at about two o'clock in the morning, a twenty-four-hour turnaround.

After twelve weeks of this routine, we believed the Miami Project could be the answer to paralysis and could possibly even help Mike regain the use of his arms and, who knew, maybe one day his legs. We rented out our house in Huntington and moved to Florida.

· · · · ·

LINDA'S LESSONS

Bob and I didn't do well in our journey together as husband and wife, but we forged an amazing partnership when it came to raising our son. We used the "together we're bigger than you" concept. It worked for us. It worked for Jace.

Juggling Jace's tough love and surviving our strange new world with all its challenges, made a positive attitude essential.

Mike and I went to Miami because we believed we would find the cure for paralysis. Believing in each other and the possibilities of life is the mainstay of difficult situations. Mike thought I could do anything. What was I going to do, let him down? Conversely, I didn't worry about finances. Mike had it covered. The people in your life will fulfill your expectations (good or bad).

Our basic expectations of our fellow man brought us through the rest. In this chapter, I mentioned the donation the airlines made to our cause. People from all walks of life came to our rescue. From bankers and hospital administrators to auto mechanics and laborers of all sorts, corporate America and the common man became our everyday angels. I have learned that positive energy is contagious, and all you have to do is look for the good in people in order to find it.

CHAPTER 9
BATHING WITH THE NEIGHBORS AND A TOPLESS DONUT SHOP

MIKE AND I KNEW THAT IN order for this relocation to Florida to work, we would have to keep his electrical equipment rented for our income. Mama and Daddy offered for us to move everything the ten or so miles to their house in Lufkin. They would make sure the equipment was safe and handle its going and coming. We agreed, feeling much appreciation, and so approximately two hundred and fifty thousand dollars' worth of equipment was moved to their place.

Daddy delighted in "getting Mike's goat," and practical jokes between the two of them were common. In fact, it was more like a contest to see who could outdo the other. Daddy wanted so badly to bungee cord Mike to water skis, and Mike was a sport, but that was where he drew the line.

The night before we left for the grand exodus to Florida, Mama and Daddy invited us over for dinner. As we pulled into the driveway, to our amazement and Daddy's glee (which was obvious by the huge grin on his face), all of Mike's equipment had FOR SALE signs posted on them! The prices were outrageously low, like one thousand dollars on a one-hundred-thousand-dollar crane! Mike started laughing out loud. He gave Daddy a nod, saying, "You got me this time, Gop!" but I could see Mike's wheels turning. There would have to be a payback! Bright and early the next morning, we were off to Florida, our next adventure, but not before Mike made sure all the FOR SALE signs were gone.

We uprooted Tiffany and brought her with us just as she was entering the fourth grade. Jace was living with his dad, and Kresta and Micah stayed with Rita in Huntington. Ready, set, go! We loaded down the little Nissan with as much as we could and hitched up a small trailer that held one power wheelchair, a manual wheelchair, and a shower chair, along with various household essentials, and headed east. Two-cylinder Nissan Sentras aren't known for their towing power, but that didn't stop us. We looked like the handicapped Clampets headed east for a cure.

The trip was uneventful, except for one little miscommunication Mike and I had.

I had never pulled a really heavy little trailer behind a relatively lightweight car. Headed down one of the really long hills on I-10, the little yellow trailer started fishtailing wider and wider, swinging the back of the car. I screamed, "Mike, what do I do?"

He yelled back, "Get on it!" He meant the accelerator. I thought he meant the brake. I stomped the brake with all my might. Car and trailer started sliding in unison until we were sitting perfectly perpendicular in the middle of I-10. I was standing up out of my seat with my foot stepping with all my weight on the brake. We jolted to a stop. I looked over, and although Mike had his seat belt on, he had slid completely out of his seat and onto the floor, scrunched into a ball. He looked up at me, smiled his Cheshire cat grin, and said, "I meant the gas." Tiffany was safely buckled in the back, and thank God there wasn't another car behind us.

We settled on Pembroke Pines, Florida, and found a small, two-bedroom, one-bath rental house located in a lower-income retirement neighborhood.

Florida Vocational Rehabilitation picked up the cost for all of Mike's treatments. Our days filled up with doctor, biofeedback, and physical therapy appointments. Literally, we were either seeing a doctor or a physical therapist eight hours a day, five days a week—finding a way for Mike to walk again was our job.

The small home was not equipped for a wheelchair, so we engineered numerous accommodations. One such modification was Mike's shower arrangements. We hooked up a garden hose to the kitchen sink and ran it out the small sliding window above the sink to the screened-in back porch so Mike could have hot water while I gave him a quick scrub-down in his plastic shower chair. I strategically placed a towel over his lap so all that God gave him wasn't hanging out, and we acted like taking a shower on your back porch in a wheelchair was a completely normal affair. No matter how quick we were, though, we never managed to get through a single shower without one of our precious elderly neighbors deciding to stop by for a chat. Mike wasn't a modest man, so it didn't bother him a bit when Alice, seventy-eight, Betty, eighty-two, and Harry, eighty-eight, came strolling over to our little back porch and drank their coffee and discussed the weather while I shampooed Mike's hair and scrubbed his armpits.

Also normal was the cheapo, five-foot, above-ground, hot-water therapy pool that we rigged for Mike, complete with Michael Don Thompsonapproved pulleys, chains, hoist, ropes, I-beams, and, of course, bungee cords. Each time we hoisted Mike up into the air, it looked like we were conducting something between a medical science experiment and bondage with all the chains and ropes. I just knew Adult Protective Services were going to come at any moment and take me away, but it was all Mike's fault. Swear to God, he made me do it! And, thanks to us, our geriatric neighbors hadn't had that much entertainment since their first "talkie."

The first month in Florida, Mike's doctor with the Miami Project used a new technology at that time—Magnetic Resonance Imaging (MRI)—and found a large bone fragment embedded in his spinal cord tissue. Unfortunately, MRI technology was unavailable at the time of Mike's accident, so this bone fragment was not detected at the onset of the injury.

One year to the day from Mike's accident, delayed decompression surgery was performed on Mike's spinal cord. We were so excited about the surgery. Mike and I both hoped he would sit up and walk off the table following surgery. It was not meant to be.

The surgery did, however, allow Mike partial use of his biceps and triceps, so that with special arm and hand splints, Mike could operate his power chair with his right arm instead of sipping and puffing with his mouth. Oh, my! Now he was dangerous! Mike and Tiffany, who was now age nine, had wheelchair races. Tiffany in Mike's lightweight manual chair, and Mike, in his three-hundred-pound power chair, turned our driveway and neighborhood street into a drag racetrack.

The summer after we arrived in Florida, Mama and Daddy, along with Jace, who had flown into Texas, made a trip to see us in their new Chevy diesel truck and fancy travel trailer. Daddy had retired, and they were on the top of the world.

As soon as Mike heard they were coming, he began plotting his revenge for Daddy's gag equipment sale. It all fell right into place as Mike and I were watching *World News* one night. A quirky story came on about a topless donut shop that, guess what, just happened to be located in Fort Lauderdale, which was less than thirty minutes from us. Mike could hardly wait till the next morning after we saw the program so that he and I could go check out the place.

From the outside, we saw a huge sign that read, "Donut Shop," but the only thing that indicated there was anything "adult" inside was a small sign that read, "No minors—must be 18 years old." Mike and I went in at about 9:00 AM to discover a neat, clean donut shop that offered no alcohol, only coffee, hot chocolate, and donuts … served by beautiful, neat, clean, young waitresses in thong bikini bottoms and no tops. There were only a few customers, and Mike and I got to have a lovely discussion with the owner about how he started such a unique establishment. We chatted for over an hour about all the famous people who had come in to have a donut and a cup of coffee served by a topless waitress. Pictures to prove his point lined the walls. We had done the reconnaissance, and Mike could hardly wait for Gop to arrive.

The first morning after Mama and Daddy's arrival, Mike casually suggested we go get donuts for breakfast. Since Daddy lived to eat, he readily agreed. Our only problem was traveling with six people who couldn't all fit into our little car. The dilemma was immediately solved by Mike, who suggested Gop ramp him up into the back of their truck, which Gop did. Our neighbor, an old, hippie motorcycle enthusiast, saw what was happening, ran into his garage, and came out with a helmet for Mike. It was shiny black with a half-naked woman on each side. Mike loved it and wore it with pride. Mama, Daddy, Jace, and Tiffany rode up front, and I climbed in the back to stabilize Mike, and for fear we would be stopped by the police. I'd surely be thrown in jail for loading my quadriplegic husband into the back of an open pickup truck.

We arrived at the donut shop. Daddy was so busy helping unload Mike and getting him safely into the restaurant that he didn't notice the "Adults Only" sign, or the fact that Jace and Tiffany stayed in the truck. Mike asked Daddy to go on in and pick out which donuts he wanted, and we'd be right behind him. Daddy waltzed in, totally unprepared for what was next. We lagged back to leave him on his own while we watched. Well, as they say, you could have knocked Daddy over with a feather when the lady wearing only a feather came breezing out to take his order. Daddy turned not red but rather purple in the face. He got this ridiculous grin and looked squarely back at Mike.

Mike was in heaven! Daddy managed an order and opened his wallet, the whole while looking up at the ceiling. He told the waitress to just take the total out of his wallet, plus her tip, grabbed the sack, and ran to where we were waiting. Mama, Mike, and I were all laughing. As we turned to leave, my sixty-five-year-old father and deacon of the Berryhill Baptist Church leaned down and whispered in Mike's ear, "You son of a bitch, I probably just paid a hundred dollars for this sack of donuts!"

Vocational Rehabilitation of Florida bought Mike his first computer in the spring of 1988. With his added shoulder and upper arm strength, little though it was, Mike, with the help of mobile arm supports and a pencil turned upside down in a hand-and-wrist cuff, was able to operate a computer and a specially adapted phone. The computer streamlined the way Mike and I paid our bills and our bank note with the income from our rental equipment back home in Texas.

Our life in Florida had a definite pattern. When we weren't on the road going through biofeedback treatments and therapy, we were doing therapy at home. But finally, after two years, Vocational Rehab had to shut off the monies. They felt Mike had made all the progress he would make. We were saddened but knew they were right.

Disappointed but still looking toward a bright future, we packed our trailer and our Nissan Sentra and headed back home to Texas, *The Grapes of Wrath* revisited.

Much to my relief and joy, Bob had "rehabilitated" Jace's attitude, and we all agreed it was time for Jace to move home to Huntington.

· · · · ·

LINDA'S LESSONS

One of the most important lessons Mike taught me was: "Linda, when you go looking for gold, don't overlook the silver." All blessings are blessings. We went to Florida seeking the cure for Mike's paralysis. We didn't find it, but Mike's delayed decompression surgery gave him enough use in his right arm to convert from a sip-and-puff device to operating his chair using his arm. Reclaiming even that small amount of use of his right arm allowed him to operate his computer and phone with greater ease. I have banned the word failure from my thought process because everything we attempt in life has one of three very good outcomes: we succeed, we partially succeed, or we learn a very good lesson.

CHAPTER 10
BUNGEE—CORD ME
TO THE MAST

OUR HOUSE IN HUNTINGTON WAS STILL rented when we came back home from Florida, and we needed the income, so we moved into Mike's empty five-thousand-square foot electrical shop building, which was located on several acres in the woods behind the house. It had no air conditioning, no running water, no bathroom, and no kitchen. It was a shop building, not a house. About the only thing that resembled living conditions was that it did have a roof, walls, and concrete floor. We slept on cots, and I even convinced the kids it was really cool to use a Coke machine as our refrigerator. Mike, being the creative electrician that he was, taught Jace how to use a blowtorch and a metal shopping cart to heat our meals.

After the first night of sleeping in the Texas summer heat, peeing and pooping in the woods, and fighting the mosquitoes, Jace proclaimed we were living in "Motel Hell!" Since this was obviously not the best of living conditions, Mike and I began to assess the expense of moving the renters out and totally remodeling the house to be handicap accessible. When we factored in the cost of remodeling and the loss of revenue from the rent, Mike decided it would be more cost-effective to build a new house. I drew a plan on a piece of cardboard box, found a building site in the woods on our eighty-five acres, and we went to the bank for a loan.

I have heard it said many times that a marriage is tested by the building of a house. Mike and I had a blast. The Christmas of 1989, I drove Mike out onto the building site and up onto the newly poured slab. Earlier that day, I had carved our initials in a big heart on a tree next to the new house slab: "LT Loves MT." Mike cried.

This incident eventually led to the writing of a book, *50 Ways to Keep Your Lover.* Mike and I tried to outdo each other doing special things and giving surprise gifts. Ultimately, I decided to share all our ideas and wrote the small book, which Mike sold to Wal-Mart stores, and eventually the rights to the book were bought and sold by Longstreet Press Publishing Company. Jace had a dream we would all be on *Oprah* with the book. It hasn't happened yet, but I loved the idea.

We had so much fun building our home that we decided to also build a speculative house to sell. A speculative house is begun without a buyer—it's a gamble. It was spring of 1990 when Mike called his business bank and they told him they were not doing speculative loans. Mike was obviously surprised, as he had borrowed and repaid millions of dollars to this bank while he was in his electrical business.

I sat down at the computer the same day and wrote a letter to the president of the bank, expressing my amazement that after Mike had done so much business with this bank, they suddenly would not loan money to a quadriplegic and a woman. It was a very sweet letter, not really a threat, and it worked. Two days later, we got a call from the bank president and were in his office that same afternoon. He carefully explained to Mike and me that the reason they were not doing speculative lending was because of the savings and loans fallout. For that reason, they had tightened up their lending practices across the board.

This was the first time I got to watch Mike do his stuff. Mike just kept agreeing with the president and asking more questions. Then Mike would get really quiet for a few seconds and say, "What if we …?" There just had to be a way to figure it out, and pretty soon, the bank president was problem-solving right along with Mike. It was absolutely amazing, like magic. An hour and a half later, we rolled out of the office with a go-ahead on our first three speculative houses.

We had a loan, so we were in the house-building business. Mike had lived in Huntington practically all his life and knew everyone in town. We called Albert, a wonderful man who had been building houses for thirty years. He taught me how to draw the blueprints to code and taught me the ins and outs of building a house. It was my job to see that the creation I designed on paper became a reality on the ground. Mike hired a secretary to work with him in the office.

After a few years, if we weren't building a new house, we were buying and remodeling an old one. Not a single day passed that I didn't learn something new from either Mike or Albert. School teacher, construction worker—you have to keep your options open and stay flexible in this old world. It was a very exciting time.

Success is not solely based on intelligence, education, family background, or even having money. A huge factor is guts, balls, cajones, ovaries! Pushing through the fear and living the dream. It is so easy to talk yourself out of trying the thing your soul tells you to do: *I don't have the money*; *I'm too old*; *the market isn't right.*

One of my favorite family stories on the subject of pushing past fear is about my Uncle Glen, my father's oldest brother, and his first job as a realtor in Houston back in the thirties. Uncle Glen was given the worst possible property to sell. To the average person it would appear that practically everything about this piece of real estate was a disaster. Uncle Glen could have been afraid and given up before he even started.

His task was to sell a small, rundown house next to a beer joint in a really bad part of town, and its only redeeming quality was a beautiful, old oak tree in the backyard. For weeks, he showed the house by driving the long way around the block to hide the beer joint for as long as possible. He'd rush the clients quickly through the shabby little house and out into the backyard to see the wonderful tree. A month later, he sold the house to a couple from Arizona who were alcoholics and delighted to have a beer joint next door. Being from Arizona, the only thing they didn't like about the place was the big, "ugly tree" in the backyard that blocked the sun, and they immediately cut it down. Uncle Glen taught me a major lesson here about not being afraid and also that "one man's shack is another man's treasure."

After about four years in the construction business, we were making really good money. We even sprung for a handicap-accessible van, engineered for Mike to ride up front. Christmas 1994, we gave the kids a special present—a trip to an all-inclusive resort in Cozumel, Mexico. The Cozumel trip was the time of my life!

I remember us all standing at the edge of the water in Cozumel. The sky was a perfect powder blue. The water was a little cloudy from a storm the previous night, but it was still okay for snorkeling. The continuous waves lapped the little wooden dock to which a fifty-foot boat was waiting and ready for a voyage, filled with tourists anxious to see the glorious reefs and abundant multicolored fish. Squeals of laughter and muted voices could be heard coming from a beach volleyball game and from the swim-up bar located behind us in the all-inclusive resort. There were nine in our group.

Mike sat in a manual wheelchair with a Plexiglas lapboard that he had engineered to hold large mugs with oversized, eighteen-inch straws, which allowed him to drink his beverage of choice without anyone's assistance. This day's mug was filled to the brim with a Cuba Libre (rum and Coke with lime). Mike's drink was safely secured with one of his ingenious inventions, which consisted of Velcro fashioned in a circle the size of the bottom of the mug and a five-inch bolt drilled through the Plexiglas and tightly fastened to his lapboard. The lapboard was tightly bound to the arms of the chair with bungee cords. We never went anywhere without lots of bungee cords. (God forbid we should spill any rum and Coke!)

Mike was shouting orders to Jace, by now a twenty- one-year-old gentle giant, who knew from years of experience handling Mike that Mike was the boss, always had been the boss, and always would be the boss. Victor, our extremely large Hispanic home health aide who had joined the group to make sure I had a vacation as well, was also taking orders from Mike. Jace towered above most people at six feet, one inch, had a broad neck and shoulders, and was very handsome (of course, I'm his mother!). Victor was six foot even and three hundred and fifty pounds of sheer lifting power. He could pick up Mike's little five-foot, six-inch, one hundred sixty-pound frame and toss him in and out of that chair like a feather.

Mike had also sprung for a ticket for Victor's wife, Lori, who although born and raised in rural East Texas, still spoke Spanish. She had a totally twisted, sadistic sense of humor that clashed with her conservative Catholic upbringing. This provided the group constant comic relief. Her imitation of an East Texan redneck nearly killed us. East Texans are a breed in and of themselves. Unlike a regular Texan drawl, we talk kind of Southern with a Cajun accent because we are located near the border of Louisiana. In other words, we made Jeff Foxworthy's imitation of rednecks sound really cultured.

Our little group included, of course, the three girls—Tiffany, now seventeen, Kresta, twenty-three, and Micah, twenty-seven. Another guy, also named Mike, from Idaho, had joined us. Jace had met him at a party several months before the trip and never even remembered inviting him, but somehow this random guy was at the airport when it was time to leave. Our family has always had a policy of "the more the merrier," so we welcomed him with open arms. That was our little group, roaring and ready to head out to sea and do some snorkeling.

The boat owner, a small, weather-worn Mexican man who spoke very little English, didn't want Mike, the man in the wheelchair, on the boat. He was obviously concerned for Mike's safety. I had the cash in my hand, and I held it out to him and said, motioning with my hands, shaking my head, and pointing toward Mike, "If he doesn't go, we don't go." Victor translated for me. Since the boat only held twelve passengers and we were nine, the boat owner immediately saw the error of his ways.

At the same time, Mike shouted out from shore while Jace held up several black straps, "Bungee-cord me to the mast!" And that is just what we did! I hope the statute of limitations is up for spousal abuse.

What an adventure we had, shopping the Mexican markets for T-shirts and other assorted souvenirs. We would swim, snorkel, and eat from eight o'clock in the morning to two o'clock in the morning the following day. We sampled all the exotic tropical drinks at the swim-up bar, laughed hysterically watching Jace and Victor try flaming cocktails, and basked in the sun until we were bright red. The entire trip was laughter, hysterical laughter, and more doubled-over-in-pain laughter. Jace and Victor could have easily been stand-up comedians. Those five days and four nights were as close to heaven on earth as it got for me.

The weekend following the trip, Tiffany, Mike, and I were walking through the Lufkin mall. As we strolled through the stores, the looks of pity from kindhearted people seeing Mike in his wheelchair was nothing new to us.

Tiffany leaned over to me after passing by one stare and said, "You know, it's really kind of funny that everyone always looks at us like they feel sorry for us, and the reality is that our family probably has a lot more fun than they do."

• • • • •

LINDA'S LESSONS

Too often people give luck credit when the credit really should go to tenacity. When we got the loans for our first three houses, I got to witness firsthand what not taking no for an answer really meant. I watched Mike accomplish this same feat again and again over the years, and I learned to do it myself.

I think most people believe successful people are never afraid. Not so! Most of us are afraid of every new endeavor and change. The only difference between those of us who achieve the things in life we set out to do and those of us who don't is fear. Put on your boots, wade through all that anxiety, laugh at fear, and beat it! If you force yourself to fight fear and beat it once, it doesn't mean you will never be afraid again. You will probably be afraid every time you face a new challenge; however, conquering the fear will be easier each time. Mike and I laughed at the fact that no matter how many houses we built or investments we made, there was always that element of fear: "Will it sell, could we lose, should the house be bigger, should the house be smaller?"

How often in life do we want to do something, but we talk ourselves out of it because we are afraid? We rationalize all the reasons we can't do it instead of just fighting the fear and plunging forward, leaving all the excuses behind. Ovaries, remember your ovaries!

"Don't worry about the mule, just load the wagon." Don't worry about all the reasons something won't work or all the ways in which you are not prepared. Just begin one step at a time, fight your fear, and do it anyway.

Another really important tidbit I have learned over the years is: don't worry about what other people think! The choices you make on this earth are between you and your creator. If you are sure your actions are in your best interest and the best interest of others, go for it! You, your guardian angels, and your creator know what is best for you. Lean on your higher power, listen for guidance, and then no matter how frightened you get, trust and do it!

Often, other people just don't have a clue what they are talking about. I guarantee if you have a bright new idea that will surely be for the betterment of all mankind, people will line up in droves to tell you why it won't work. Pray and listen for answers from above, not here on earth. If you have a burning desire to publish your poetry, Aunt Edna will joyfully tell you all the reasons it won't sell—even if she can't read. Even the most loving influences in your life may discourage you for fear you'll be disappointed. Nothing is as disappointing as not trying. I have always told my children I was very proud of them when they didn't win. Loss was evidence of trying!

Ultimately, we are not judged by financial success or failure. We are judged by the way in which we treat those who pass our way. So, if you are a quadriplegic, make it your goal to walk no matter if the critics line up for a mile, because in your efforts, whether you walk or not, your heroic endeavor could inspire another.

CHAPTER 11
OUR FAMILY, IT'S ALL TRUE

WHEN MY SPIRITUAL ADVISORS AND I were in heaven planning this lifetime, I'm sure I told them, "Okay, I'll volunteer to be married to a quadriplegic, but I'm not going down there without Tiffany."

Tiffany was my rock. There's no doubt we had more fun than any family I know; however, being the caregiver for a quadriplegic took a toll on my mental and physical wellbeing. Micah was unable to help much because of her own disability. Kresta was busy being a teenager, and after she graduated from high school, she threw herself into work and college. Jace was with his dad in Idaho for years. I couldn't have made it without Tiffany. Even as a small child, she loved taking care of Mike, spending time with him, changing the TV channels, feeding him, and working in the office with him.

One of Mike and Tiffany's favorite adventures was "mud hogging" in the woods. As a little girl, Tiffany would ride on the back of Mike's power wheelchair while he drove in high gear with his mouthpiece. Mike taught her to drive a backhoe at the age of eight. At eleven, she learned to drive the stick-shift Nissan Sentra backwards around our circle driveway while Mike timed her. Mike adored Tiffany because she wasn't afraid to do anything he told her to do. At nine, he taught her to type by instructing her how to place her fingers on the keys, and then he would dictate business letters for her to type for practice. By the time she entered typing class in high school, she could type faster and more accurately than the teacher. When Tiffany turned sixteen, Mike taught her to play craps and even devised a way to get my under-aged daughter onto the floating casino riverboats in Louisiana. I can still hear the conversation on our first family trip over to the boats, and I still can't believe I let them go through with it as Mike divulged the criminal plan.

"All right, Tiff, your mom's gonna hang back while you and me go up to the boat together. When it's time for you to show your driver's license to the guard, I'm gonna throw myself into a 'spasmatic' fit and you're gonna have to make sure I don't 'hurt myself.'"

An injury to the spinal cord causes, among other things, horrific spasms, which usually have to be treated with high doses of muscle relaxers, but even a slight touch can set off a spasm. They are pretty scary looking!

Mike grinned his naughty grin and continued, "They won't even ask to see your ID, and they'll just walk us on the boat cuz they'll be too worried about me to even think about asking if you're old enough to get on."

My sweet sixteen-year-old looked and acted like she was twenty-five, and if Mike told her it could be done, she didn't hesitate. Well, sure enough, it played out exactly as Mike planned, and those two rolled right onto the boat. Mike caused himself to go into spasms by jerking his head and shoulders enough to make his entire body start to involuntarily shake and go into extension. The poor security guard thought Mike was going to die, and of course, Tiffany, who was also a natural actress, calmly said to the guard, who was about to call for a medic, "Don't worry about it, sir, my daddy will be just fine if I can just get him over to the side and get him some water. Mind if we just roll on inside so we don't cause a scene or bother the other guests?"

Flustered and concerned, the guard said, "Well, of course, ma'am. Why don't y'all come right over here to this private area and relax until you're able to enjoy the boat. If you need anything, please let me know."

That guard never thought once about asking for her ID. I was watching the whole scene from afar with my stomach in knots. Within a couple of minutes, I saw Mike's body stop its spasms. The two partners in crime soon rolled over to the craps table, where Tiffany began changing dollars, placing chips, and rolling dice per Mike's instruction. They were a team.

Tiffany thought Mike hung the moon and absorbed every word he said and every skill he taught her. Mike never considered Tiffany his stepdaughter.

In his mind, she was his. And although Tiffany had a relationship with Bob, Mike was the man who raised her and who helped mold her into the confident adult she became.

Tiffany was the reason I could occasionally steal away and get a haircut or go to the grocery store. Sleep deprivation was a battle I fought daily due to Mike's nighttime regimen. He had to be turned over regularly to avoid bed sores. Because his body temperature was unregulated, all night long the fan had to be turned on and off. Tiffany made it possible for me to take the occasional life-sustaining nap.

When Tiffany began the sixth grade, though she weighed less than eighty pounds, she and Mike had developed a system whereby she could even transfer him into bed. He simply drove his chair up close to the side of the bed. Tiffany yelled, "*Timber,*" pushed his shoulders and the top half of his body over sideways onto the bed, and then jumped onto the bed and pulled his legs over into place. The two of them figured out this little trick while I was at the grocery store one day. When I arrived home from shopping, they were laid up side by side, heads inclined, both with legs crossed, watching TV, and giggling as I came into the bedroom. I was astounded.

As many times over the years as I tried to relay to Tiffany the depth of my gratitude to her for being my salvation, only another caregiver could understand my appreciation for her helping hand.

So much happened to our family in those years while the kids were growing up. Kresta was eighteen when we discovered she had Type I diabetes. She was in and out of the hospital, constantly trying to get her sugar levels under control. She was also diagnosed with a rare disease called Glycogen Storage Disease. Just like her father and sister, Kresta rallied her strength, and in spite of her illness and trips to the hospital, worked two and sometimes three jobs.

Unstoppable, diabetes and Glycogen Storage Disease didn't keep Kresta from getting her boobs. The mustard seed didn't work! Every family get-together, year after year, we had to have a huge discussion about how and when Kresta would get her boobs. Now, lots of kid's parents take them to the bank for a loan for a car or a college education. With Kresta, her priority was breast augmentation. As soon as she was twenty-one and had a job to make the payments, she and Mike loaded up in the van and went to the bank. It didn't bother Mike in the least to roll right into the office of our commercial banker, Keith, and tell him he wanted to cosign for his daughter to get titties! Mike, always the money manager, knew it was a good way for Kresta to establish her credit.

The kids, their needs and wants, Mike, and the business consumed our daily lives, but I was not the only caregiver during this crazy period. Mama was struggling to care for Daddy, who had developed Alzheimer's.

Denise's husband, Greg, was diagnosed with brain cancer at age thirty-six. Surgery had removed the cancer—and much of Greg's reasoning abilities. Denise joined Mama and me in the caregiver role.

Before I knew it, I was getting Tiffany ready to leave for college. She was accepted to the University of Texas at Austin and was excited about the opportunities that a larger city and huge university had to offer. After her freshman year, she got a job as a resident assistant (RA) in Jester Residence Hall.

One day, after her first staff orientation, I got a phone call from Tiffany. She explained she and fifteen other RAs had to sit in a circle and introduce themselves, giving a description of their families. When Tiffany's turn came, she began:

"I'm Tiffany Cordell from Huntington, Texas, a very small place with just one traffic light. There were eighty-eight kids in my graduating class. I was raised by my mom, Linda, and Mike. Mike is my stepfather. He is a quadriplegic, paralyzed from the shoulders down from a car accident." The group issued appropriate "Oh nos."

Tiffany continued, "But he is amazing, brilliant, and funny. He and my mom build houses together. My mom, Linda, is my hero. She takes care of Mike 24/7, runs the house and the building crews, works with Mike in the office, and she still managed to attend every school function I was in." The group responded with "Wows" of admiration.

"I have two stepsisters. Kresta is a Type I diabetic and has a rare disease, Glycogen Storage Disease. It's where your liver doesn't work properly; it's a slow form of starvation." Looks of shock crossed the faces of the group. "Micah, my other stepsister, was in a car accident at sixteen, just six months before Mike's accident." Now, looks of horror were exchanged among the group listening to Tiffany's description of her family. "She has a head injury and can't talk." Tiffany's fellow RAs had looks of sadness and disbelief on their faces. "My brother, Jace, is twenty-three and was born with only four toes on his left foot." Now the climate of the group changed. They began to try to smother giggles, thinking this was a sick joke.

"My grandfather has Alzheimer's, and he recently paraded nude in front of four of my closest friends. My Uncle Greg had a cancerous tumor removed from his brain a few years ago, and now he has no short-term memory and loses things a lot, including himself."

At this point, Tiffany's audience was beginning to laugh overtly, thinking Tiffany had the most sadistic sense of humor they had ever heard. Tiffany, having grown up in a family who would rather laugh than breathe, was enjoying the reaction immensely and brought her oration to a close with, "My mom, my aunt, and my grandmother all suffer from depression and are on antidepressants. And that's my family!" Tiffany's finale brought howls and giggles, but when the laughter slowed, one girl managed to get out, "Tiffany, you shouldn't kid about stuff like that!"

With a huge smile on her face born of wisdom far beyond her nineteen years, Tiffany proclaimed, "It's all true!" It *was* all true, and as pitiful as it sounded, let's face it—we were a mess. We had to laugh at ourselves because if we didn't, we'd sit around crying. There was never a dull moment, and as the kids got older, they had no problem inviting their friends to join our dysfunctional but uproariously entertaining family.

Several years after we built our home, we designed and installed a gorgeous ten-foot-deep ramped pool and hot tub, which was quite a step up from the above-ground pool we had in Florida. We didn't have to use pulleys, chains, and hoists to get Mike into this pool. Mike was always in his electric power wheelchair, which meant we would have to transfer him into a manual chair so we didn't electrocute him if he wanted to go for a swim. Transfers from chair to chair could be taxing on my back, so Mike eventually suggested we avoid a transfer into a manual chair by chunking him in the deep end. We did! Mike would hold his breath, I'd toss, and Tiffany would dive down and pull him up. If Tiffany happened not to be home, Mike would hold his breath, I would toss, and then I'd jump in to save him. This took trust to a whole new level.

When there's a pool, there's a party, and oh, did we have some great times, especially around July 4, when we had an annual Hawaiian-style pig roast.

We went down to the local butcher and got a whole entire pig, head and all. We injected it with all kinds of spices, oils, and rubs and then wrapped it in the giant banana leaves that grew like tropical weeds around our pool. Before burying it in a five-foot long, three-foot wide, and four-foot deep hole, it would have to sit on ice while the fire pit grew hot enough. Then we would bury it and let it roast for twelve hours until we dug it up and feasted on the meat that fell off the bone.

One infamous pig roast took place the same day that I also agreed to host a wedding for one of Tiffany's good buddies. Now, why, you ask, would someone host a pig roast and a wedding on the same day? Well, the wedding needed to take place quickly, as the bride was *very* pregnant. To say her father was holding a shotgun would be an understatement.

So, we'd have a wedding and a pig roast! We'd make sure the wedding was in the morning, hours before the roast, and no one would be the wiser. The thing we didn't account for was the frozen, bloody, stiff, dead pig that Jace had brought in the night before and placed in the guest bathroom. In all

61

the hubbub of getting ready for both the wedding and the roast, I completely forgot about the evening's main course lying on ice in the bathtub in the bathroom that the bride and groom's parents, grandparents, aunts, uncles, and cousins were all using. It didn't dawn on me until the bride came up to me after the wedding and said, "Linda, thank you so much for letting us use your house for the wedding. I know it was a lot for you to take on, especially with the pig roast happening tonight."

Then she leaned in close and confided to me with a giggle, "Mother (The bride's eighty-two-year-old grandmother) fainted in the bathroom after seeing the dead pig. We just scooped her up and gave her a glass of water, and she finally came to. I didn't want you to worry about her if she seemed out of sorts. The pig just took her breath away, that's all."

I was mortified! How could I have forgotten about the damned pig! Had I realized it was in the guest bathroom, I would have moved it to the master bath!

Animals were a constant in our life. Living in the Piney Woods, we always had lots of dogs and critters running around the place. I mentioned to Mike one day that I had always wanted to have peacocks because I just thought they were beautiful. On my next birthday, Mike surprised me with three baby peacocks. We built a large wooden and chicken wire pen back behind the pool.

Two of our best friends, Denis and Diana, called the pen the Raddison because it was so fancy. The Raddison was twenty feet in diameter and octagonal in shape. Well, it was supposed to be octagonal. Denis, a professional carpenter, helped me build it while Diana served food (she was the best cook in East Texas) and Mike bossed the job. When we finished, I counted and there were only seven sides. Mike blamed Denis, and Denis blamed Mike, and the peacocks never seemed to care.

Mike never did anything in a small way. Now we had this huge pen for just three peacocks. It seemed like a waste of space, so Mike called the forest service and had our land designated as an official wildlife refuge. The next thing I knew, Mike had located an animal rehab organization, which had a bunch of squirrels that had been extracted from people's attics in Houston. He talked Jace into loading him up in the van and driving them to pick up these animals, which were apparently in need of rehabilitation. Rehabilitation generally meant returning them safely to the wild. On their way home, Jace called to report on their status. I started laughing the minute I heard his voice.

"Mom, this is a pretty serious situation." His voice was grave. "One of these squirrels is wearing an eye patch and has a peg leg, two are crack heads, and the other three are hardened coke addicts."

The next few years, we had every kind of animal imaginable coming and going, from squirrels to deer. Sebastian, our baby deer, walked in and out of the house at will, using Mike's motion-activated door opener. He delighted in following me into the bathroom, where we visited while I tended to my call of nature. Gives that phrase a total new dimension, doesn't it? The squirrels were especially fun, as Mike delighted in training them to eat off his lapboard. We always seemed to lose sight that our job as rehabilitators was to return them to the wild, and instead we invited them into our home. And when we tried to turn them loose, they wouldn't leave. We almost lost a secretary once (our office was in our home) when a squirrel decided to take a leap from the file cabinet onto her head. We came to realize her sense of humor was somewhat different from ours. In our house, only the strong survived.

In addition to animals, our home was always a place of refuge for the kids and their friends. Of all the strays that walked in and out of the door, Veronique won the award for most totally freaked out by our wacky world. She was a young French woman who Tiffany had befriended while at the University of Texas. Veronique was touring the states and ended up in Austin. She had run out of money and needed a place to stay. Tiffany invited her to come back home with her to Huntington for the summer. We quickly renamed her "Vero" and began the process of overcoming the language barrier. Even though East Texan is sort of Cajun and Cajun is kind of French, we didn't speak French, and although she'd been in the States for a while and understood English, Vero had never heard or seen anything like us.

Vero must have thought she had landed in the local zoo with all the animals and birds roaming around the place. Mike and I were going ninety to nothing, busy building houses and running jobs, and we often forgot to eat. Poor girl nearly starved to death. We typically forgot to eat breakfast, grabbed a sandwich for lunch, and finally, around seven o'clock, we got around to a decent dinner.

After about a week of this pace, Vero said to us in her sweet, cute, innocent French accent, "This family is so busy. You don't eat. Aren't you hungry?"

We all felt very guilty, realizing the French were known for their good food and good wine. I told Vero in the typical mom voice I used with all the kids who frequented our home, "Sweetheart, you are welcome to anything any time. Never go hungry. If you can find it, you can have it."

Vero responded with a big smile and hug for me. Mike also had a suggestion. He said, "Vero, when you get hungry, you just come up to me or Linda and say, 'Hey, y'all, I'm so hungry I could eat the ass end out of a menestratin' skunk.'"

Vero didn't have a clue what Mike was talking about, so for the next ten minutes Tiffany tried to explain what he had just said. When the light dawned, Tiffany and Mike made her repeat and practice the phrase, which turned into Vero saying through tears of laughter, "I sooo hongry, I could eat hass end of menstruation skunk."

No matter what we were doing or who was coming or going, our home was the place for fun and a feeling of acceptance. Regardless of who you were, where you came from, what baggage you had, or how strange or not normal you felt, our family had a way of making even the strangest souls feel the most welcome. We became a revolving door for old friends and new faces. As the kids got older, I never knew who was going to show up, who would stay the night, or what I would find in the morning.

On my forty-eighth birthday, Mike and the kids decided to have a party for me at the house. One of Jace's best friends, Michael, showed up in a chicken costume playing a guitar. It was a wonderful night with lots of friends, laughter, music, board games, swimming, and tons of great food. Our kids were all grown, and it was Mike's and my tradition to go to bed early, around midnight. It was also my tradition to wake up early before Mike was up in order to steal a little alone time—just me, my cup of coffee, and a stroll around the tropical garden that surrounded the pool. The morning following my party, with coffee in hand and stepping quietly over pallets of sleeping bodies, I tiptoed out the French doors that led out to the patio, pool, and hot tub.

The sun was blindingly bright. I covered my eyes and took about three steps, which brought me to within about ten feet of the hot tub. My eyes had adjusted to the light, and lying face down before me, totally naked, sound asleep, and floating on a plastic raft in the hot tub, was Michael minus the chicken suit. At that instant, Jace stepped out the back door and quietly came to stand by my side. Placing his arm around my shoulder, Jace began the dialogue in hushed tones so as not to awaken Michael, "He has a nice ass, doesn't he, Mom?"

"Yes, hon, he does."

"Well, see, Mom, here's the deal. Since I'm in college and I didn't have any money to get you a present, I got you a naked boy for your birthday."

We then exchanged quiet giggles, a big hug, and I said, "Thank you, son, I'm goin' for my camera." I got a couple of really good shots before Jace went in and woke everyone up so that they all could see the naked boy Jace got me for my birthday.

Nakedness? I was always too self-conscious for public nudity. But with us, nudity wasn't taboo because it wasn't ever associated with sexuality. The nakedness that happened from time to time in our lives was always associated with the ridiculous, the outrageous, the funny, and the sublime.

Tiffany was the most conservative of our bunch, but she made up for it with her selection of men. After she graduated from UT, Tiffany found a technology job in Austin and started dating a bartender named Chris. The weekend they moved in together, Tiffany asked the entire family to come help them unpack and move furniture into their new, little place.

Mike, Jace, Kresta, Micah, and I all piled in the van and headed to Austin. By this time, we had all met Chris, but we weren't sure he was right for Tiffany. Chris still hadn't proven himself worthy of our baby girl. When we got to their new house in Austin, Tiffany and Chris were livid because they had been waiting for hours on a used appliance dealer to deliver a "slightly-used," ten-year-old refrigerator that they had paid eighty dollars for. They were poor as church mice, so not getting the fridge, or not getting the money back, were not options.

The salesman refused to pick up the phone when Chris called, and it was becoming apparent that the shyster was not going to deliver the fridge. Chris made it his duty for eight hours straight to call and leave messages every fifteen minutes. First, the calls were polite yet stern: "Sir, you were supposed to deliver our fridge two hours ago. Where are you?"

Then, Chris thought he could make him feel guilty: "Sir, we'd really appreciate it if you'd bring us our refrigerator. My girlfriend and I are broke and can't afford to lose eighty dollars. Plus, that fridge is needed for my girlfriend's sister, who is a diabetic and has to keep her insulin cool."

When that didn't work, his calls began to have a different tone. "Look, you son of a bitch, I know where you live, and if you think you're gonna screw me out of eighty dollars, you're ridiculous. I'm a trained and lethal kick boxer (he wasn't), and I've got my girlfriend's brother here who's six-one from the backwoods of East Texas, where they kill wild boars for fun (that's true), and I've also got my best friend, who's half Polish and half Dutch, six-seven, and was taught how to fight from his father who was on a chain gang in New York (true too), and, finally, I've got a totally psychotic electrician who can easily shut down the electricity to your entire shitty used-appliance shop (he didn't mention Mike couldn't move a muscle), all ready to descend upon your ass. So you either bring me my damn money at seven o'clock in the morning or you're gonna wish you had never fucked with me!"

After Chris hung up the phone, he sheepishly looked at all of us and said, "Ummm, how'd that sound? Think he'll believe it?"

We all simultaneously let out a loud battle cry: "RRRRRRRAAAAAA!" We would have followed him into hell all for the sake of a used, eighty-dollar refrigerator. The scene was priceless. If that salesman had been a fly on the wall, he would have seen Mike loving every minute of it and rocking the only thing he could—his shoulders—back and forth as he sat in his wheelchair drinking a "rummy," Micah limping off to the bathroom with her awkward gate, Kresta giggling as she injected insulin into her thigh, Jace pumped and ready but far more of the lover than fighter, and then Wayne, Chris's best friend, who was as huge as Chris said but lived and died for the online virtual game EverQuest, and the only thing Wayne had fought for years were online goblins and druids.

We all went to sleep that night together, camped in the middle of the living room because Chris and Tiffany still didn't have any beds! At seven o'clock on the dot the next morning, the doorbell rang. Chris jumped up off his pallet, stripped stark naked, marched straight to the front door, swung it wide open, and without so much as a hello, demanded, "Where's my money!"

The gritty, few-toothed refrigerator man was so caught off guard by Chris's exposed member that he reached into his eggshell paint-splattered pocket while awkwardly maintaining eye contact, and handed Chris eighty dollars in cash. Before Chris could say anything else, the shady appliance salesman turned around and ran as fast as he could back to his pockmarked, dented '92 Ford Ranger.

We all cheered for our victorious and business-savvy streaker, who had just gained the entire family's approval. Tiffany had found a keeper!

Our life on a rollercoaster took us high, and then there was always gravity. On March 29, 1998, my father, Warren King, died after a ten-year struggle with complications from Alzheimer's disease. My mother, Bessie, strong, brave, and tenacious, had kept their lifelong promise never to put each other in a nursing home. They made their journey on earth this lifetime together to within one month of their fiftieth wedding anniversary.

· · · · ·

LINDA'S LESSONS

It is all true. Our life was fraught with challenging situations, but the silly, wild escapades and ridiculous family moments are my treasures. Whenever I try to decide what to give to someone I really love, I usually choose a gift that makes a memory.

My daddy, Warren King, was responsible for some of the most glorious memories of my life. His abundant sense of humor and ability to roll with any disappointment paved the way for me to see my life as a joyous adventure. I know he now walks in a place where he can keep an eye on me when he isn't eating a hamburger with God. My mother's heroism continues to be my shining example.

Chapter 12
Why? Where? How?

After years of moving back and forth between Bob in Idaho and me in Texas, Jace decided the thing he loved to do most was work with people and make them laugh. He figured a career in healthcare would allow him to do both. He attended Angelina College, right up the road from our place, and got a degree in Respiratory Therapy. I was so proud of my brilliant, funny son. He had come so far. The things that came out of his mouth were absurd, but regardless of whether you were a child or a senior citizen, you fell in love with him.

I've never known anyone who could make friends as quickly as Jace. He could be in a room with a catfish farmer, an African diamond smuggler, a little person, a lady of the evening, or a fire fighter, and within five minutes each one of them would think that he hung the moon. Then, he'd turn around and invite them to go with him to the Renaissance Festival or a tractor pull, and I guarantee each one of them would load up and go right along. Jace had friends who were gay, while others were conservative Catholics. Race or religion didn't matter to him. He never judged. Jace just did his best to get along.

One of Jace's best friends, Kenny, loved to tell the story of a late-night confrontation he and Jace had in the parking lot of a convenience store their senior year of high school. In Kenny's words:

"Jace and I are both pretty big. I'm six-four and have worked hard all my life. Jace is only six-one, but the boy is wide and strong as a bull. Well, we were coming in from a party one night about one in the morning and stopped at Nuway for a Coke and some of those fried Crispitos. We walked out the door into the parking lot toward our truck sittin' at the gas pump, and four mean-lookin' dudes—must have been from out of town cuz we didn't know 'um—walked up to us and started jerkin' our chain. Just startin' shit. I've always liked to fight, an' I figured with the size on Jace an' me, we could probably take those four assholes. I looked over at Jace to make sure he had my back, and Jace sits his drink an' sack of Crispitos on the pavement. He starts turnin' red in the face and slobberin out his mouth. He's starin' off at nothin' in particular and starts wavin' his arms around and snortin' like a Javelina pig. Foam starts comin' out his mouth like he's havin' a seizure or somethin'. The four dudes actually started lookin' kinda scared, and so I started playin' along. I said, 'Jace, don't do nothin' crazy, man!' With that, Jace started screechin' real loud and jumpin' up and down real high while he continued to wave his arms, and snot started runnin' out his nose. Now, these four guys had begun to look plumb white, and I screamed over the loud noises Jace was makin', 'Damn, Jace, don't kill 'um!' All four turned and ran as fast as they could to their car and drove off. Jace and I looked at each other, started laughin', and both of us got down on the concrete and hollered. When we both finally got our breath back, stood up, and picked up our Cokes and stuff, Jace turned to me all apologetic and says, 'Kenny, I'm sorry, I just don't like to fight, and you're a crazy son of a bitch, because those bastards would have kicked our asses.'"

Jace would barrel in the front door and sweep me up in his arms, no matter what I was doing. He always gave me big hugs and kisses and called me his "Little Lumpy Dragon," a bizarre pet name he branded me with when he was ten. He always started in with his sick, sadistic humor, which would make me laugh—the kind of laughter where no sound comes out of your mouth and the muscles in your stomach tighten so hard you are physically in pain, and if sound could come out of your mouth, you would tell him to stop, but you can't, so you stop breathing and turn red, and eventually your brain triggers a gasp for air so you don't pass out.

One afternoon, I looked up and saw him coming through the front door. I ran over to him and hopped up into his arms, proclaiming, "Jace, I screwed the undertaker!" All the kids knew that one of my pet peeves was the high cost of funerals. I continued, "Mike and I have called the University of Texas at Galveston Medical School, and we are donating our bodies to science! You kids won't have to spend a dime, and the funeral homes won't get a penny." Jace put me down, and we sang and did the "We Beat the Undertaker" dance to the tune of "Who Let the Dogs Out? Who, Who, Who!"

Out of breath, we fell on the couch, and Jace said, "Yeah, Mom, that's really cool. That's just what I want to do, too, and then I want everybody to have a wake on the beach, and I want there to be hookers, and midgets, and fire trucks, and I want everybody to get naked and party their asses off!" And then he got really gross and said, "Mom, and just think how funny it will be when you die and your corpse is delivered to the lab, and it will have filled up with gas, and just about the time some young med student is bending over the table to cut into you, your body will fart, or move, or twitch, or something and scare the crap out of him!"

Jace's humor was being put to good use on a daily basis at a local hospital as a respiratory therapist. He charmed his way into the hearts of his patients, brightening even their darkest days. Jace decided that, having gotten a job, it was time to build a house. Mike and I had promised all our kids that if they would get their educations and keep their credit clean, as soon as they got a loan, we would help them build a house. Jace did just that. He got a loan with Mike and I walking him through the process. All of our subcontractors pitched in, and we built Jace a small, three-bedroom, two-bath brick starter home. Next, he bought his dream car, a brand new Honda Accord EX V6 two-door coupe, black on black. He ordered special plates: LMFAO. He called and told me now that he had a house and a hot, fast, new car, women were falling out of the trees. Jace had arrived.

It was during this time I began having dreams—very bad dreams. I had never been clairvoyant or psychic in any way that I knew of, so I didn't worry too much. I just assumed it was something I ate. I started having a reoccurring dream of massive car accidents, one car after another crashing, and bodies lined up by the dozens. And then I had a dream that our whole family was having a picnic on the side of a tall, grassy hillside. We were laughing and having so much fun, and then I stood up and walked away from the family. A woman joined me, but I couldn't see her face. We watched in amazement as the sky turned to blood—a thick, dark red drape of blood slowly descended from the heavens. We both knew, although we said nothing, that it meant the end of the world.

On December 17, 2000, at 1:30 AM, I received a call that Jace had been in a single-car accident. It was nearly freezing and misting rain that night. He had been driving fast on a small, backwoods logging road less than five miles from our house. A highway patrolman reported passing him, and he had clocked Jace doing around one hundred miles an hour. The caller at the scene said he took a curve too fast, left the slick highway, and flew head-on into a large pine tree. The caller told me Jace was in an ambulance headed to the hospital. Her tone sounded ominous. I didn't ask questions. I was afraid to.

Tiffany had come home from Austin for the weekend, and she and I were up late talking when the call came through. I called my mother and asked her to come over and stay with Mike while Tiffany and I went to the hospital. Tiffany grabbed my keys and got behind the wheel.

She asked, "Mom, do you want me to speed?"

"No," was my simple answer. I began to pray. Tiffany and I simultaneously reached across the front seat to hold hands as we drove the twenty terrifying minutes to the hospital. Thoughts raced through my mind. I saw the anguish and struggle Micah had to face every day with her severe head injury, and yet I couldn't stand to lose my precious, funny, wonderful son. It was unthinkable.

I began to pray for both of us. "The best for Jace, the best for me ... the best for Jace, the best for me ... the best for Jace, the best for me." This mantra I crooned nonstop until we pulled up to the back emergency entrance of the hospital. I reached toward Tiffany. She put her arms around me, and I prayed aloud, "God, please put your hands on us and get us through whatever we have to face."

Upon entering the ER, we were escorted to the "quiet room." My heart sank. I instantly knew if Jace were in emergency surgery or all right, we wouldn't have to enter this room with its soft lighting and a hospital staff person assigned to greet us and sit by our side while we waited for a doctor. I felt my life drain out. I knew undoubtedly what was coming. For about fifteen long, excruciating minutes, the three of us—Tiffany, me, and this strange woman sitting to my left—said not a word. I felt like an animal caught in a trap. I desperately wanted to leave, run away, and never have to hear what they were surely going to say. I began to panic, and then I began to pray silently, "God, put your hands on me. I don't think I can do this."

A doctor entered the quiet room. He was dressed from head to toe in white. My mind said, "The angel of death." The doctor looked down at me and said, "Are you the immediate family of Jace Cordell?"

I couldn't move my mouth to respond. Tiffany said, "Yes, we are."

The doctor continued, "Jace was pronounced dead at 2:00 AM due to injuries sustained from the accident."

Words then flooded out of my mouth. "Can his organs be donated?"

"No," the doctor said in a whisper.

I continued, "His body is to be sent to UT Medical School in Galveston and donated to science. There will be no burial."

Tiffany, just twenty-two years old at the time, took my face in her hands, looked me in the eye, and said, "Mother, you will not have to do a thing. I will handle it all."

I collapsed in her lap and began to sob. The woman to my left, the stranger sent to help me through this, laid her hands on my back. I felt an energy, like a magnet pulling me toward her. I sat up, and as I looked into her eyes, she placed her hands on either side of my head.

Tears began to stream down my face, and I said to her, "Your hands feel like God's hands."

Tiffany escorted me to see Jace's body one last time. He was so beautiful. I remember thinking his face was remarkably normal considering he had been in an automobile accident. I later found out that his left arm had been almost severed, and that he had gone headfirst through the driver's window, but none of that showed when we viewed his sheet-wrapped body. I remember being afraid to touch him. I'm not sure why. It sounds crazy, but I said nothing aloud to him. I just sent him a message telepathically: "Jace, we did all right this time around. I love you."

Tiffany stood silently, tears streaming down her cheeks. I turned to her, and we left. I felt my knees give, and she grabbed for me.

Jace, being a respiratory therapist in the area, had many friends and coworkers in the hospital on duty that night. One of Jace's coworkers at the hospital, Jeff, who was also a therapist, was waiting for me to come out. I think Jeff and Tiffany caught me before I hit the floor. In my semi-lucid state, the vivid dream about the end of the world I had just weeks prior streamed through my mind. I now knew its meaning. Our world, the one where people laughed, had fun, and enjoyed life no matter what, had surely just ended.

It was all something that could not possibly be happening to *this* mother. Tiffany got me home that night. Denise, Mama, and I think many other people were waiting when we returned home. I remember some of their faces, but nothing they said mattered or made sense. I took no phone calls. I received no guests. Tiffany and Mike took care of all the arrangements. They were ever vigilant in their commitment to getting me through this. I cannot imagine how parents who lose children and have no support system get by.

We had a memorial service in our home three days after Jace died. Since his death was in December, I decided the wake that he had mentioned just weeks earlier, the wake that I never in my wildest dreams thought I would be planning, would need to be postponed until warmer months. However, the service needed to be a tribute worthy of who he was, so Chris bought about fifteen sweatshirts and ironed on each of them Jace's notorious catchphrase, said at every gathering Jace was ever a part of: "Here's to Hookers, Midgets, and Fire Trucks!" Regardless of who Jace invited to a soiree, he made sure it was known that anyone could come. He could be inviting the president of the United States to one of our get-togethers, and Jace would say, "Sir, you must be there. There's going to be hookers, midgets, and fire trucks."

Did all three ever show up? I don't think so. That phrase just let people know it was going to be a great time and for people to check their inhibitions at the door. It was Jace's way of saying everyone was welcome.

Yes, even I wore one of the sweatshirts. Jace's coworkers, friends, and family listened to his favorite music, everything from Johnny Cash to Bob Marley to Metallica. And we told stories, so many Jace stories that the service lasted all day and into the night.

After the memorial service, my amazing family and friends checked on me from time to time to make sure I was "okay," but eventually they had to go back to their own lives. It wasn't their son that died, it was mine. Mike, Tiffany, and the secretary picked up the entire workload of the construction business. I would periodically wander into the office, not knowing how my job was being handled, nor did I care. Eventually, Tiffany had to go back to work.

For months, I slept day and night in our garage loft. The only times I left my seclusion was for the necessary care I had to do for Mike. By this time, we had hired home health aides who could assist with many of Mike's needs, which allowed me to remain in my hideout, where I would sleep, sleep, and sleep some more. I would awaken with songs playing in my head. For example, about three months after Jace's death, I woke up one morning and found myself looking directly at a picture of Tiffany and me. The song playing in my head was: "Love the One You're With," by Steven Stills.

Grief clung to me like mud. Every day brought a new layer of thick, grayish goo, which threatened to choke off my breath. I could barely get out of bed. The weight was so heavy I found it difficult to walk. I knew instinctively that I had to fight this suffocating substance, and it was at this point that I asked for help. I had read about meditation and visualization, but I didn't know the techniques. I simply sat down on the soft carpet in my quiet loft with my legs crossed and turned everything over to God. I closed my eyes and began to sob. My body shook, and tears streamed down my face. When I could breathe well enough to speak, I simply said out loud, "Please help me."

With my eyes closed, I saw a colorless mist with streaks of light and dark. After a few moments of quiet, I saw movement, and a shrouded form came toward me. It was a woman in a heavy, dark purple velvet, full-length cloak, which also covered her face. In my mind's eye, I could see me sitting there like a cocoon covered in thick, gray mud. Bright golden light beamed down on me like a spotlight. The woman lifted a beautiful translucent green pitcher from out of nowhere and began to pour sparkling light-filled green liquid on my head.

As she poured, chunks of mud rolled off me, and I began to see the top of my head, golden and shining with light. She continued pouring, and mud ran in wet streams from my face and down my neck. Soon my face began to sparkle and was crystal clean. The magic green fluid continued to pour from the pitcher with an infinite bottom, and huge pieces of the dark substance broke away from me each time to reveal a perfect, crystal-clean part of my body. As the mud flowed away from me and hit the ground, it magically dissipated into golden light. As soon as I could see more and more of myself, I realized I was a child sitting naked with my knees tightly hugged to my body, my face hidden, looking down into my lap. Long, golden blond hair streamed down my back.

When all the sludge was gone, I raised my head and looked toward heaven. I stood up, and beautiful light illuminated me. I was clean. I still could not see the woman's face, but now she was kneeling on the ground. She reached out to me with a soft, thick, dark purple towel. I walked to her. She wrapped the warm, safe cloth around me and pulled me into her lap. Her arms held me close. Mother God rocked me.

In time, I began to read dozens of life-after-life books and slowly began to develop a philosophy of what life on the other side was like. I had a desperate need to know what life after life really was. Until Jace died, I had given lip service to heaven and God. But now, it was paramount for my own survival to discover what happened after the body died. I needed to know where Jace was and what he was doing, not for the purposes of knowing whether his soul was "saved" or if he was in hell or purgatory. I had to know my son was somewhere else, thriving, so that I could continue to live on earth without him—knowing I would be with him again.

The books I chose were written over a span of twenty years by physicians, psychotherapists, religious masters, hypnotists, and mediums. With each book, I kept seeing the same messages repeat over and over again.

We plan our lives before we come to earth. We plan our challenges around the lessons we need to learn. Once on earth, we have choices to make as to the paths we will follow. If we choose not to learn the lessons we intended for this lifetime, we will simply choose to come back and try until we succeed. The occasions in our life that feel the most painful are actually an avenue for the greatest growth. Loyalty, patience, generosity, strength, honor, wisdom, and love are qualities learned over many lifetimes and because of many trials.

Why do bad things happen to good people? Bad things happen to *all* people. It is the nature of the course we are taking here on earth. Often, God is blamed for the hard time we are having. Not true. Our creator has given us free will to learn at our own speed and has given us backup in the form of spirit guides who are with us always to gently nudge us in the right direction.

Journey of Souls by Dr. Michael Newton is a compelling, scientific study and a detailed explanation of what happens to us when we die and what our spirit lives are like on the other side. Although I learned from every book, I really connected on an intellectual and spiritual level with *Journey of Souls*. Dr. Newton's book answered all my questions regarding life after life and allowed me to picture where and what Jace was doing, and even how he connected back to me here on earth. *Journey of Souls* gave me much peace, and it provided the foundation of information I needed to begin to heal.

Five months following Jace's death, we had a special service at Galveston Beach for what would have been his twenty-seventh birthday. Friends, coworkers, and family gathered together in and around a beach house we rented. There were tents and campers lined along the beach for a quarter mile. All who came brought a tribute of some sort to help us celebrate Jace's life. Some got naked and swam in the ocean as their tribute, some dressed as stripper fire fighters, some brought their guitars and sang, and others simply cried. I wrote a poem.

MY SON IS DEAD

*The morning sun comes screaming through my window, "Get out of bed!"
I scream back, "Shut up. Leave me alone! My son
is dead." I pull the covers over my head.
The people come, the things they say, "Be strong, be brave, he hasn't
really gone away.
He's at peace, time will help …"*
Shut up. Leave me alone! My son is dead. I pull the covers over my head.
There is nothing you can say, there is nothing you can do. Unless … you
cradle me in your lap and rock me gentle, say no words but rub my head
and kiss my cheek and let me cry and scream and weep. Hold me tight if
you dare and pull the covers over my head. My son is dead. My son is
dead.
One week, two, three weeks, four. I wander out my bedroom door. I love
my daughter and husband, so I get up. But I'm pissed, I'm scared, and
I'm ready to fight. It's God I'm gunning for.
My God, God, are you out of your mind? How could you ever be so blind,
so thoughtless, so unkind?
You're brutal, you are mean, God, you're out of control. Have you looked
down lately into this black hole? Do you have me confused with someone
else because I have done my best … there's no one else who has given
their all and smiled the whole way through like I have done. You don't
care about me. I don't care about you.
It's been one month, two months, three months since Jace died, and I'm
afraid. Is my son all right? Where is he now? Because of the things
I've taught Jace, is he in trouble somehow?
I taught Jace God is love; he should have no fear. There is one God, one
God for all. I taught him to be a Christian, a Buddhist, a Hindu, a Jew—
there is no wrong way to worship God. That's only a few.
On the other hand, I was taught to fear God. Was I wrong? They must be
right. He has punished me, and my son, is he all right? Where is he
tonight?
Four months now … Jace has been dead. My fear is overwhelming. I got
on my knees. Send me an answer, God, I need your help. Please. God, I'm
begging. Is my son all right? Where is my son? Send me an answer.
Where is Jace tonight?
God, you must have the answer, no one else does. Are you full of anger, or
are you full of love? Where is my son? Where is Jace tonight? Give me
an answer, is my son all right?*

God spoke: "I love you," he said. "I always will. There is nothing you could do or not do and I would love you still. I never punish. I never judge. I only love. You are my child."
And then God said,
"You are on a mission, and Jace was too. You both planned this life yourselves and your death, as all people do. Jace fulfilled his contract. His work was done. He left the darkness of earth and he came home.
You're lonely for him but only for a brief moment. You will spend many more lives together. You will share the epiphany of joy and the depths of sorrow together, and each time you finish your work and gather your wisdom, you'll come back home. Back to the vision of ..."
And then God described heaven, and he told me how Jace was. "First off," God said, "Jace is not at peace or even close, nor is any part of heaven, for that matter, since he has been home.
As soon as Jace remembered he could fly, he began taking children flying. He's Peter Pan. He's Peter Pan, the man with the plan. 'If I can fly,' says Jace, 'anyone can.' And so now Jace and all the children fly everywhere they go. It's caused such a ruckus, I just don't know. And Jace's music and dancing," God continued, "is loud as can be. He's gathered them all. They've all come to see ... Mama Cass, Janice Joplin, and Jimmy Hendricks are three. Bob Marley, Buddy Holly, Otis Redding, and Elvis ... You can see ...
Jace has planned music night and comedy night too. With Jace, Chris Farley, Belushi, and Radner, I really just don't know what to do." And then God began to laugh and laugh and laugh, and tears filled his eyes. "That Jace is a wonder," he said. "It's no surprise ... you miss him like you do.
His mission on earth was to make you laugh and everyone else too. His life taught the importance of living life to the fullest, dancing every dance, and taking every chance. Jace accomplished his job. And then he came home."
God finished ... and I fell to my knees and began to sob and kissed God's feet and the hem of his robe. "Thank you for taking care of my Jace for me, God, until I get to come home. What can I do, God, to help you? I'll do my best, God, show me the way." And then God lifted my face and told me this that day:
"Linda, my child, just tell people not to be afraid of me ever. They should never fear me or death, for there is no death. No one ever dies. Hell is the pain and suffering you go through on earth. But each and every problem you face makes you stronger and gives you wisdom.

You are experiencing life for me, my child." God said, "So share
your love and light with all you meet. Be kind.
That is all there is to it. Never fear
me. You will always do your work and then come home.
No one ever dies."

As I have said, I was always too self-conscious for public nudity. With tears streaming down my face and sobs wracking my body, I managed to read the poem, and then I stepped out of my clothes and walked into the ocean. It was Jace's last request. How could I deny him?

· · · · ·

LINDA'S LESSONS

Jace could make me laugh like no other person in this world. He laughed— oh, how he laughed—and he gave the gift of laughter to everyone he was ever with. Jace danced at every party. Often, he was the only man on the dance floor. Don't pass up the dances of your life. Don't worry about looking silly. Don't worry what others think. Just love from the bottom of your heart. And dance the dance of life.

I would like to take this opportunity to thank the authors of the many life-after-life books I read during those long, hard months, for I truly believe that, along with my family and with messages from the other side, these books are the reason I kept my sanity and survived the loss of my precious son. I am especially indebted to you, Dr. Newton. Thank you.

Chapter 13

Messages from the Other Side

Most people left the Sunday following Jace's wake, but Mike, Tiffany, and her college roommate, Laura, and I stayed the rest of the week. Jace's birthday fell on Tuesday of that week, and I needed to be at the beach on his actual birthday. Per Jace's wishes, we donated his body to the University of Texas at Galveston Medical School. His remains were cremated and distributed into the Gulf of Mexico. Just as people mark a special occasion by making a pilgrimage to the cemetery in which their loved one is buried, I needed to be there at the Gulf on Jace's birthday, looking out into the vastness of the ocean, knowing that his spirit and wishes were being carried out.

That same night, a bird flew into the beach house. The house had high ceilings, and it took us fifteen minutes to finally catch the bird. Tiffany had it in her hands and offered it to me. Holding it gently, I stepped outside onto the deck, facing the ocean with its sound of the eternal in-and-out motion of the waves washing the sand. There was a full moon and a gentle breeze as I opened my hands to free the frightened little creature.

We all sensed there was something special about the visit from this tiny, little sparrow because Mike, Tiffany, and Laura all quietly followed me out onto the deck for the release. When I opened my hands, expecting him to immediately seek freedom, he instead hopped onto my index finger. For the next sixty seconds or so, the little bird hopped sideways, back and forth on my finger, looking at me as if he was anxious to tell me something. I began to cry, and as I looked over my shoulder, I could see my family crying also.

It was then that I noticed the little bird had a wound on the top of his head. During his accident, Jace had gone headfirst through the window on the driver's side of his car. I began to sob quietly, and then it occurred to me what he needed to hear. I began talking to the bird.

"Mother loves you so much. I understand you have to go. Please stay in touch with me. I love you, and I know you love me." And he flew away.

For the next few years, we received messages regularly from Jace. The next one came five months later, on Halloween, the day of the dead. Jace's sadistic sense of humor is very prominent in his afterlife. Tiffany and her friends had gone to a Halloween party, and Tiffany was the designated driver. On their way home from the party, they decided to stop at a fast food place. Pulling into the drive-through, Tiffany lowered her window, called out their order, and drove around to the pick-up window.

The cashier inside handed Tiffany their drinks and then held out a separate, smaller Styrofoam cup and said, "Here, we thought you should have this." Tiffany had never met, much less seen, the girl cashier and was quite shocked as she took the small cup that was obviously filled with something other than liquid. Tiffany looked in it and gasped when she saw a small, brown sparrow. The girl in the window explained, "That bird flew into the window a few minutes ago, and we caught it. We thought you should have it." She never said why they decided to give the bird to a random customer, but Tiffany knew why.

That night, Tiffany called me from Austin and told me the story of Jace's visit.

"Mom, as soon as we got home, I went straight out to the backyard, turned on the porch light, and gently turned the cup sideways on the ground. He did the same thing he did at the beach house. He just hopped around on the ground for a minute or two, and of course I began to cry, and then I started to talk to him. When I finally said, 'Thanks for coming, Jace. I'm doing okay. I hope you are too. I love you,' he flew away."

The holidays following Jace's death were a nightmare. Not only would we be celebrating the holidays without Jace, but December 17, 2001, was the first anniversary of his death. The Grinch didn't have anything on me. Like all families who have to get through seasonal and celebratory events without the person who should be there and isn't, we survived, but we were so grateful when the holidays were over.

Grief is a process you walk through day by day, head down, like a plough horse against the wind, but when a special occasion comes around, the pain is a garbage truck unloading its whole load on top of you. It was during this time that I received another message. It was not a bird. One of my dearest friends, Melody, came to stay with me. She was Jace's age and had a similar taste in music—heavy metal—and she told me she had a CD I just had to hear. My nerves jangled when she played it (remember, I'm an old person). I graciously listened to the song, not understanding a word. At the same time, I somehow knew that Jace wanted me to know what the song said. I asked

Melody for the CD cover so that I could understand the words to the song. To my amazement, the lyrics of "Parabola" from the *Lateralus* album by Tool are an unbelievably beautiful tribute to the eternal nature of spirit and the fact that "All this pain is an illusion."

We survived the holidays, and in February, I drove to Houston to stay a week with Melody's mom, Darlene, who was having a hysterectomy. Darlene had been my college roommate and one of those wonderful people who had held my hand and allowed me to cry on her shoulders many times following Jace's death. On the way to meet Darlene in Houston for her surgery, I suddenly had the feeling that Jace would somehow contact me through Darlene's surgery. When I arrived, I told Darlene that I felt Jace would deliver me a message through her surgery. She reacted with very little surprise, as she is a very spiritual person and knew Jace had already sent us messages on several occasions.

Darlene responded, "I'll do my best." The surgery was long but went well. I met Darlene in her semi-private hospital room in recovery after she awakened from anesthesia. For the next three hours, I sat in the corner reading while Darlene slept. During that time, I had time to observe a wonderful young woman, the aide who darted in and out, caring for Darlene and the other person in the room, taking blood pressures and temperatures. This aide was lovely and had a barely concealed giggle and a huge smile on her face. Each time she entered the room, she would smile and joke, quietly and carefully, using humor to help in the healing process of her patients. It made me think of all the comments Jace's coworkers had made at his memorial about how he could light up a hospital room and that no matter how sick the person, Jace could always make them laugh. I felt compelled to tell the aide what I was thinking, but I knew I would start crying, so I kept quiet and read.

Finally, Darlene stirred and woke up. Upon seeing me, she immediately began to apologize. "I am so sorry, Linda, but I didn't get a message. From the time they knocked me out till about now, I don't remember a thing."

"That's all right," I told her. "I'm just glad your surgery went well. I must have gotten my signals crossed." About that time, our little aide entered with her flashy smile and a plastic ice water pitcher with a lid. Darlene carefully and slowly sat up in bed, took the pitcher, and began to open the lid to take a drink. But she stopped in mid-air, mouth open.

"Oh, my gosh, Linda, here's your message!" I jumped up and walked over to her bed to see what she was talking about. Darlene was pointing at the room number that had been written in permanent marker on the top of the pitcher lid. If you looked at the lid upside down, the hastily scribbled, handwritten room number, 228B, formed the cursive representation of the letters J-a-c-e.

I began to cry while Darlene explained to the aide that my son had died, and this was his name on the pitcher lid. At that point, I figured I might as well tell the aide what I had felt compelled to tell her all morning.

Over my sobs, I managed to get out, "I have been feeling like I should tell you all morning … You are doing the right thing in life by making sick people happy with your wonderful personality. My son was a respiratory therapist and he, too, used his funny personality and quirky sense of humor to make people in the hospital feel better through laughter."

The aide stared at me wide eyed and said, "Wow, you just answered a question for me. You see, I already have a degree in accounting, but I began working in the hospital as an aide because I knew I wasn't in the right field. Just this morning, I stopped by to pick up the paperwork to sign up for the respiratory therapy program here. I have been wondering if I am making the right decision. You and your son just told me I am."

I have thought many times since that day how much we are all one. A total stranger received a message she needed to hear through a message I received from my son on the other side. The link we have to one another is unmistakable.

Three months after Darlene's surgery, Jace's birthday, May 23, came around again. After Jace's death, his birthday was always the hardest day of the year for me. By this time Tiffany had begun working south of Houston and had purchased a little house near the bay. That particular year, I wanted to spend his birthday alone, with him. Tiffany said she was going to be out of town on Jace's birthday and that I was welcome to stay at her house. I got a sitter for Mike and headed to her place to be in solitude and near the water.

On the three-hour drive, I talked to Jace as though he were in the car, explaining that we were going to celebrate his birthday together and that I expected to learn some really cool stuff from him. After all, he had been on the other side for a year and a half by now, and he should know all the answers. I told him I didn't want to know any small potatoes stuff. I wanted to know the answer to the big question—"Why are we here?"

Rounding the corner to Tiffany's house, I passed a seafood restaurant with a big sign out front that read, "Best Oysters in Texas—3 Years in a Row!" Well, Jace and I both love oysters, so I decided that was where we would have dinner. At about seven o'clock that night, I headed up the street to Gilhooley's Restaurant.

Tiffany had called earlier that evening to check on me, and when I told her Jace and I were going to Gilhooley's, she said, "That sounds great, Mom, but don't go in there and sit by yourself. Sit up at the bar and visit. Some really nice people work there."

Gilhooley's is one of those best-kept secrets. It's a little, out-of-the-way place down by the bay, with plywood floors, a tin roof, and some of the best home-cooked food in South Texas. I walked in and, like Tiffany told me, stepped up to the U-shaped bar and ordered a large iced tea and Oysters Gilhooley's.

While I waited for my meal, a tall, lanky young man with his hair tied back in a ponytail sat down at the bar across the corner from me. His skin was dark and weathered, indicating he was someone who worked outdoors. He had a nice smile, and we ended up striking up quite a conversation. We began discussing house building in the area, as he was a construction worker too—a framer. My meal came out with hot and steaming oysters on the half-shell, broiled in butter and garlic, with shrimp and cheese and yummy spices on top. My construction worker friend and I continued our conversation over dinner, and soon we branched off into a more philosophical discussion. Ultimately, as I was being served hot, homemade apple pie and coffee, I asked him what he thought we were on this earth to accomplish.

Without a second's hesitation, he answered, "That's easy. It's all about electrical impulses. Our bodies emit positive and negative energy. It is our job here on earth to send positive energy to every person we come in contact with."

For years now, I have thought about my meeting with the young construction worker and the message he brought me. Never a day goes by, nor does a person cross my path, that I don't attempt to fulfill his directive, because I believe without a doubt he carried Jace's answer to my question— why are we here?

· · · · ·

LINDA'S LESSONS

To all those who grieve for a person who has crossed over the invisible veil, it is my fervent desire that if this book accomplishes nothing else, it serves as reassurance that every time you hear her voice in your head, see the butterfly he sent, or listen to a song on the radio that reminds you of them, *you aren't crazy!* They are reaching out to you. Never again doubt or feel embarrassed to tell it or to believe it! Your loved one is there!

Over the years, I learned so many important lessons because of Jace's death. One of the most important is that there is really very little in this world that is worth worrying about. Jace's death gave me the freedom to know that, in comparison to his loss, very few things matter. The flat tire, the tenant who doesn't pay, the dirty house, and on and on; none of the small things that we freak out about are really very important. I have begun asking myself, "Will that even matter ten years from now?" If it won't matter ten years from now, it is not worth fretting over.

A couple of weeks ago, I sat in a doctor's office reception area, waiting for my annual checkup, when a man about fifty came stomping into the room. He was red-faced and furious about being stuck in traffic. He went into a ten-minute tirade about how he hated traffic, other drivers, and being in the city in general. The thoughts going through my mind as I listened quietly to his enraged discourse were: "Wow, what a lucky man. He has obviously not had anything really bad happen in his lifetime that he could think a traffic jam was so horrible."

The most important thing I have learned in this lifetime comes from Jace's message from the other side. Each day I live on this earth, I attempt to send a positive message to each and every person I contact. I believe that envisioning light, love, and laughter for everyone raises the vibration of enlightenment throughout the world. If my positive thoughts can impact my own life—and I know they do—then why shouldn't they impact others in the same way? Just as every atom in my body is a part of me, so are we, each person, a part of the *one*, and thus we can each affect the other. We each have a purpose. Can you imagine how the world would change if each of the billions of people on our planet simply sent positive energy to each and every person they contacted?

CHAPTER 14
A BEGINNING

AFTER JACE LEFT THIS PLAIN, I felt the laughter had gone out of my world. But we had Chris, and in 2003, Tiffany married her precious, handsome, brilliant, extremely funny soul mate. They were married on a Galveston beach with a wonderful reception, great friends, good food, and magical music and dancing. I kept expecting a bird or at least some sign from the other side. It didn't happen. For me, their wedding was a fabulous occasion because Tiffany had chosen the man I had always prayed she would.

Earlier, I wrote that in the first few months after Jace's death, I would awaken with song lyrics on my mind. Often, the lyrics I heard were, "There will be one child born in the world to carry on," from the song, "And When I Die," by Blood, Sweat & Tears. It was at Tiffany's wedding that I knew why I often heard those lyrics in my mind. Tiffany was my one child left on earth who would continue our family.

Following the reception, Tiffany and Chris left for a glorious honeymoon in Hawaii. When they returned, Tiffany called to share all they had seen and done, and then I could tell she was crying. She told me how Jace had visited them.

She said, "Mom, he was there. Jace was there. I really thought he would be at my wedding, but he decided to hang out with us on our honeymoon instead. I still can't believe it. When Chris and I walked into our room in Kauai, the balcony doors were open. We put our bags on the floor and looked up and saw a beautiful bird sitting on the desk in our room, just staring at us. I looked at Chris and we laughed, and then we just started talking to the bird as though it were Jace. We had a five-minute conversation, and then he nodded his head and flew out the balcony doors."

Jace sent a bird to wish Tiffany and Chris a wonderful life and another to proclaim a new life. By the time of Chris and Tiffany's wedding, Mike's health had severely declined. He had developed cardiomyopathy, a form of heart disease, due to all the medications he had to take, and the steady flow of rum and Coke added to the decline. I asked Mike what he felt he still had to accomplish in this life, fully expecting his answer to have something to do with business.

He surprised me by saying, "All I have left to do is have a grandbaby." Just a few weeks following our conversation, Tiffany and Chris told us we were going to be grandparents. Mike and I were both ecstatic. When Tiffany was five months pregnant, she and Chris invited Chris's mom, Jenny, and me to the ultrasound appointment (Mike was too ill to travel), where we found out whether we were having a boy or a girl. The ultrasound showed that this baby was as lacking in modesty as the rest of our family. There was no doubt we were having a baby girl.

When Jace and Tiffany were in their teens, Jace had told Tiffany he was going to name his first kid Sky, regardless of whether it was a boy or girl. At his death, Tiffany promised that she would carry out his wishes with her first child.

As Chris, Jenny, Tiffany, and I watched our little baby girl on the monitor and listened to her rhythmic heartbeat, Tiffany said, "We all love you, Sky Olivia." Olivia was the middle name of my grandmother, Lola Olivia.

A baby girl! There was only one thing to do: go to Babies 'R' Us, a gigantic store filled with anything and everything new parents could possibly want or need! We had to have little girl clothes! Tiffany and Chris went to register for all the myriad things they would need once Sky arrived, while the grandmothers went berserk looking at the cute, tiny pink baby girl clothes and all the wonderful baby furniture.

About thirty minutes later, Chris walked up behind me and put his hands on my shoulders. He whispered in my ear, "Have you seen him?" and pointed up. Yes, sitting directly above my head on a giant metal beam in the far back corner of the store was a little bird looking down at us.

• • • • •

LINDA'S LESSONS

Pain is what we may choose to use for infinite growth. A new family, a new baby is the meaning of infinite. When something happens to us in life that feels like the end of the world, we can always be assured if we will just wait a little while; we will always discover renewal. Jace's death left a hole that can never be filled, but a new grandbaby is a great way to enlarge the heart!

Chapter 15
The Last Windmill

MIKE BEGAN TO LOSE HIS MEMORY the year after Jace's death. Our secretary confided in me that Mike had called to talk to our banker and an hour later tried to call him back regarding the same issue. Mike became paranoid about our bank accounts as he realized he didn't remember balances as he once had. This turn of events broke my heart and his. We always called Mike "the money man." He could keep bank account numbers, important financial information, and phone numbers miraculously tucked away in his mind. Mike's mind was essentially all he had since he had no use of his body. He always said, "When my mind is gone, I want to be gone."

Four years earlier, when Mike was diagnosed with cardiomyopathy, doctors told him the only thing that may prolong his life a few years before he went into congestive heart failure was to give up his rum and Coke.

On the ride home from that doctor's visit, Mike asked me, "Babe, do you think those docs are right about the rum? What do you think I should do?"

I responded, "Mike, this has to be your call. I signed on to be your arms and legs, but I won't make your decisions for you. I've never been a quadriplegic. I've never sat in that wheelchair. I know if it were me in that chair, I might need rum, crack cocaine, and a very large hammer to live out each day. There's no judgment here, my love. You do what you think is best and, like always, I'll support your decision."

By the winter of 2003, Mike's appetite was gone. He drank protein drinks and took vitamins. For the first time in his life, he didn't have the desire to get out of bed. His body was slowly breaking down, and he developed a pressure sore. Home health saw him daily. I drove myself crazy trying to do more to turn around a downward spiral. I knew we were facing the end of our journey in this lifetime together. I began to pray over and over, "Please, God, let him have no fear, no pain, no fear, no pain."

Each day, Mike would ask the same questions over and over and over, sometimes as many as thirty or forty times, usually questions regarding our bank accounts. Patiently, I tried to answer each time, and when the frustration level got too high, I would simply crawl in bed next to him and we would cry together. I was losing my hero, and there was nothing I could do to stop it.

Mike had highs and lows. His health would plummet. I would call the kids home, and he would rally. He began seeing beings around him. One day, when Tiffany had rushed home because I thought it was the end, Mike asked her, "Hey, Tiff, do you see those people over there in the corner dressed in white?"

And then he began to recite Psalm 23:4: "Yea though I walk through the valley of the shadow of death, I will fear no evil ..." In all the years that I had known him, we never went to a church service, nor had I ever heard him recite a Bible verse.

We went through so many ups and downs, so many false alarms, thinking he was going to die. The third week of August of 2004, he made a drastic turn for the worse, and I asked all the kids to come home. Sky was just seven weeks old. After the kids got in, Tiffany placed Sky Olivia, Mike's only grandchild, on his chest while he slept. The sound of his heart and his deep, rhythmic breathing rocked his baby granddaughter to sleep. It was his final accomplishment. At two o'clock in the morning on August 17, 2004, Kresta, Tiffany, and I laid next to him while he died. There seemed to be no fear and no pain. He was so loved and admired by so many.

Once again, our home served as the place for our friends and family to say their final goodbyes. Mike loved Willie Nelson, and so Mike's best friend, Dwan Coleman, did the eulogy with "Pancho and Lefty" playing as background music. Tiffany and Kresta each got up and told stories of their funny, brilliant, and brave father. I read the song lyrics to "The Impossible Dream" and explained that Mike was my Man of La Mancha, the dreamer of impossible dreams. He was the man who had loved me, been my best friend, and taught me so very much. Mike's body was donated to science, and his ashes were sent out to sea.

• • • • •

LINDA'S LESSONS

In the eighteen years I lived with Mike's paralysis, there was never a single incident where he took his hurt, anger, frustration, or pain out on me. Near the end, there was a time when I was weak and tired, and once I lashed out at him for something he did not remember. I still carry the guilt that I could not be strong all the way to the end like he was. A caregiver carries scars as deep as the sick loved one. At Mike's death, my feelings tumbled one after another like wet clothes in a dryer. At times I felt relief, then guilt, and then anguish at losing my best friend—then free and then guilty, and then lonely, so lonely. My hat is off to the caregivers of our world, the gallant men and women who silently wage their war of devotion with little or no reinforcements and no hope of relief, save their own death or the death of the one they love.

Insurance reform should include backup for the caregiver.

CHAPTER 16
DIVINE INTERVENTION

FOR THE FIRST MONTH FOLLOWING MIKE'S death and memorial service, I think I wandered around the house, lost. Every nook and cranny was a memory. Now that I had all the time in the world to sleep, I couldn't. For the first time in nearly twenty years, I was not someone else's arms and legs. I was no longer a caretaker and had all the time in the world to take care of myself, but the time became a curse.

I hated feeling sorry for myself, which had never been a part of who we were, so I decided it was time for a move. I needed a fresh start. I began readying myself to rent the house and move down to the bay to be closer to Tiffany, Chris, and Sky. I felt guilty leaving Micah and Kresta—abandoning ship—but they understood my need to be near Sky.

Within three months, I was packed, had put nonessentials in storage, and was ready to relocate and begin looking for a place to buy or a lot on which to build. Tiffany and Chris graciously allowed me to move in with them for as long as necessary, but I knew they needed their privacy, so I asked if I could move a small, used travel trailer onto their property while I built my new home, and they agreed.

Building my new house in a new location was great therapy for me, as depression was my constant companion. Staying busy was the only thing that kept it at bay. I had to find all new contractors and learn from the ground up how to build a house to windstorm specifications, since hurricanes regularly impacted the area. Hard work was the ticket, along with the blissful hours I spent with my kids and wonderful grandbaby girl.

I was extremely interested in energy conservation and in learning all the new ideas on the horizon, so I attended an energy conference in San Antonio. It was one of those conferences that you leave feeling pumped with excitement. I learned so many new ideas regarding the best way to insulate and build a home while keeping in mind air quality and phenomenal energy efficiency.

The first night in the motel room in San Antonio, I called Denis and Diana. I was crying when they picked up the phone. I explained that I was at this conference and had learned so much, and all I wanted to do was share all these new ideas with Mike. I missed him so much. As best friends do, Denis and Diana listened patiently with sympathy. The next morning as I was getting dressed, my cell phone rang. By the time I put down the hair dryer and got to the phone, I had missed the call. To my amazement, the name in my caller ID was Mike. Mike's cell phone was carefully packed away in a storage unit. I was the only one with the key.

Within six months, I was in my new home, just five miles from Tiffany, Chris, and Sky. The construction process had been challenging in a new area with new contractors, but I was very proud of my little house by the bay. I had downsized and built a small, three-bedroom, two-bath brick home just minutes from the water. Time and new surroundings had helped me to get through the worst of my grief, I thought. I was wrong.

As soon as my busy schedule slowed down, more depression set in. I knew the symptoms well. During the eighteen years of being Mike's sole caregiver, my doctor eventually put me on Prozac. My precious children teased me about my antidepressant, and for Christmas one year, Kresta even gave me a large, ceramic cookie jar-shaped container with "PROZAC" written in large letters across the front. I displayed it proudly.

I had rarely taken drugs of any kind. I was very fortunate and was always a very healthy person. But, at about ten years into our marriage, sleep deprivation and the mental and physical demands of being a full-time caregiver finally took their toll. I threw a full plate of food at the wall of our bedroom after an acquaintance in the grocery store told me I looked like I was gaining weight. I followed up the culinary disaster by sitting balled up in the fetal position in the corner of the room, crying uncontrollably. None of this was characteristic behavior for me. It scared the hell out of Mike, too, who sat looking on without even a way to put his arms around me. After about ten minutes of hard sobbing, I composed myself, put Mike and I both to bed, and was on the phone at eight o'clock the following morning, making an appointment with our family doctor.

My doctor told me that, under the circumstances, he was surprised I hadn't been throwing food for years. (I was losing my mind, and I had a doc with a sense of humor.) He then proceeded to explain that our brain makes a neurotransmitter called serotonin, which produces a calming effect, but it cannot make an unlimited supply. Under normal circumstances, when life is rolling along as it should, the brain makes enough serotonin to keep our mental state on a normal keel. If, on the other hand, one's life is stressful for any number of reasons (work, illness, relationships, etc., etc., etc.), the brain may not be able to keep up with the demand.

My doctor put me on an antidepressant, and for several years I rocked along with very little emotion at all. I didn't cry or fall to pieces, but I also didn't feel real joy, either. It was like the antidepressant had cut off both extremes of emotion. I had too many folks counting on me to worry about it. Then Jace died. Something told me I needed to experience the grief. I don't think it was very smart, but I went off the antidepressant cold turkey. What it actually amounted to was that right after he died I was barely eating or drinking anything anyway, and by the time I even thought about my antidepressant, a month had rolled by and I didn't care. I now understand that the pain I was able to feel was the open door of my spiritual journey.

A year following Mike's death, the classic symptoms of depression returned: feelings of hopelessness, weight gain, insomnia, and lethargy plagued me. I couldn't sleep, and I could barely get out of bed. While in bed or out, I was also having menopausal symptoms, including night sweats, and to make matters worse, I seemed to be allergic to everything on the planet. If I wasn't on an antibiotic, I had a sinus infection. My nose ran nonstop. Illness, grief, and depression tied me to my bed like the straps of a straightjacket. Depression is not something one chooses. It is like an evil fungus that crawls its way into the soul and then feeds on the mental and physical body until the "you" that was once there is gone.

I was depressed, but I finally decided that perhaps *depressed* was what I *needed* to be for a while. I have always believed that all unfolds as it should, and my going through this horrific depression had to have a reason. I began to be thankful for my depression, to lean into it, feel it, and know it was with me for a very important reason.

Even when I was barely able to get out of bed, I still felt driven. There was something really important I needed to be doing. It was only a whisper in the back of my mind: "You should be doing something to help others." I now know I experienced this time in my life, this relentless depression, so I could share how I beat it!

In the haze of this dark hour, I felt compelled to write and started working on a book—or at least tried to write it, time after time after time. Everything I wrote sounded flat. What did I have to give? And yet, I felt like my writing a book about my experiences (being a caregiver for an incredible human being who happened to be quadriplegic; our amazing, wacky, and bizarre family; the horrifically painful loss of my son; and the physical, mental, emotional, and spiritual repercussions of it all) was what I was meant to do. I know it sounds nuts, but I almost felt like there was a boot between my shoulder blades, like this book was my destiny, and yet, through the haze of my depression, I kept asking myself, *Why on earth do you think you can write a book when you can barely get out of bed?*

It was at this point that I received an e-mail from my cousin, Dianne. Dianne and I are only seven months apart in age, with me being the older. She has always had the habit of introducing me as her older cousin! Dianne is one of my closest friends and a person I could discuss spiritual matters with on a really special level. Dianne lost her sister, Debbie, in a totally bizarre auto accident. She empathized with the grief that came with the loss of a loved one who seemed too young to die.

Dianne's e-mail was an invitation to a seminar. The topic was, "Talking to Your Angels," with the discussion being led by psychic/medium/author, Kim O'Neill. I was immediately interested, but I unfortunately already had a commitment for that time slot. I did, however, get online and go to Kim's Web site. I was impressed with everything Kim had to say on her Web site, and so, the next day, I went out and bought Kim's book, *How to Talk with Your Angels*. I couldn't put it down. The basic message was that we all have guardian angels. They are with us at all times, helping us negotiate our time here on earth. If we reach out to them, help is on the way.

Bright and early the morning after I finished *How to Talk with Your Angels,* I did just that. "Hey guys," I said, "I think you want me to write a book. I need all the help I can get, so here we go." That morning, I began again to write my life story. For three months, I transcended my depression, and although it never really left, I knew I had a mission and was not going to allow anything to stop me. By the time the holidays rolled around, I had pretty much written the story of my life, love, and loss, but I felt defeated. The story had no impact; how could it possibly make a difference? I shut down my computer and walked away.

During the holidays, I stopped writing and did my best to count my numerous blessings and enjoy my precious kids and, of course, my granddaughter, who was by now two and a half. What a joy, what a delight, what a bright, shining family and baby girl I had. Although I knew I had so much left to be thankful for, something in me still felt dead and hollow. Those of you who have dragged depression around like a ball and chain know the feeling I am describing. No matter how hard you try to convince yourself to get better, no matter how fortunate you know you are, something blocks your light, making it impossible for the real you to come shining through. When I returned home after spending most of the holidays with Chris, Sky, and Tiffany, I faced an empty house, myself, and the depression.

One morning about a week after New Year's, I opened my eyes, and when my feet touched the floor, I could hear Mike in my head. The words shook me to the core. He said, very plainly, "I died so you could live."

Tears filled my eyes, and I answered him with my whole heart, "I will. I will find a way to begin to live again. I will find my joy and be happy again." I thought about Mike's plea all day. That evening, Kim O'Neill's advice popped into my head, and I knew that "all I had to do was ask." Immediately, sitting on my bed, I began talking to my angels.

"Please, guys, help me. I can't seem to fix this depression myself. Show me how. Please show me how!" I immediately felt lighter. I had no idea how they would help me, but I knew I would receive an answer.

$$\bullet \ \bullet \ \bullet \ \bullet \ \bullet$$

LINDA'S LESSONS

I have discovered that our guides truly are always there, and by asking for their help and then actively listening for an answer, it is uncanny how fast they can reply. I was in the garage one day, and since I am intuitive and not organized, I couldn't find the charger to my screwdriver. I smiled, looked toward the heavens, which in this case was the garage ceiling, and asked, "Okay, guys, where's my charger?" Immediately, I had the feeling I needed to look in the catch-all drawer in my kitchen. Sure enough, there it was.

CHAPTER 17
SHE'S BACK

ONE WEEK AFTER I SOUGHT HELP from my guides, a friend gave me the book, *Hormones, Health, and Happiness* by Steven F. Hotze, MD. That night, I read almost all night long. Page after page, Dr. Hotze was describing me: sleeplessness, night sweats, allergies, constant antibiotic use for sinus infections, mood swings, food cravings, weight gain, zero energy, and *depression*. I have always been one to seek out natural solutions to medical problems, but after reading Dr. Hotze's book, this seemed like a no-brainer. I was convinced that since the contents of this book had described me and my symptoms perfectly, depleted hormones was an accurate diagnosis. But, did I want to take hormones made from natural yams and soy beans or a synthetic concoction made from pregnant horse urine? "Well, *YES,* I think I'm gonna go for the yams and soy beans." The next morning at eight o'clock, I made an appointment with Dr. Hotze, whose offices were in the Houston area, about an hour from where I lived.

The doctors and nurses at Dr. Hotze's clinic were exceptional. I was treated with great care and respect. They ran blood work, did allergy testing, prescribed bioidentical hormones and supplements, and put me on a yeast-free diet to rid my body of candida, which is a condition one gets from (among other things) taking antibiotics regularly.

Within weeks, my menopausal symptoms were all but gone, and the allergy drops had given me the first relief from sinus infections I had experienced in years. But, best of all, without the use of antidepressants, *my depression was over*. Replenishing the body with hormones *made from natural substances like yams and soy* treated the cause of my depression, not just the symptoms. Time and stress had robbed me of life-sustaining hormones. With their return, I not only conquered my depression, but I regained my strength and energy and was relieved of all menopausal symptoms. And guess what else? For the first time in my life … I had a raging libido! Yes! Yes! Yes! Hormone balance had changed my world!

By the middle of February, I started working on my book again. As I was reading it over, I was amazed. I thought it was pretty good. The words hadn't changed; I had. As it turns out, hormones aren't just for teenagers, they're really important for old people too! I got back to my book, and now the words that had been crawling on the page began to flood. I was writing and laughing, loving, and feeling blessed and joyful. Linda was back!

· · · · ·

LINDA'S LESSONS

In the years following, I would learn so much more about the need for a lifetime of hormonal balance. I have since learned that young and old alike can have hormonal imbalances. Bioidentical hormones have treated everything from depression to infertility to sexual dysfunction to menopause and andropause symptoms. I have learned that our hormones are necessary not only to make us feel better, but to keep us healthy. For example, testosterone is used by every muscle in the body in men and women. What is our largest internal muscle? Our heart! As we grow older and our hormones become depleted, our bodies begin to basically fall apart. We get diseases like cancer and heart disease. Bioidentical hormones play a huge role in helping us to ward off these diseases. Now, mentally recall all the television commercials obviously geared toward all of us Baby Boomers that feature antidepressants, antidepressants to assist the antidepressant, high blood pressure and cholesterol meds, heart medication, constipation aids, drugs for osteoporosis, and products to correct erectile dysfunction. We can continue to treat the symptoms, or we can treat the cause.

But the elderly are not the only age group that can fall prey to hormonal imbalance.

In today's world, young people have so much stress due to work, parenting, and so many other responsibilities, and stress plays a huge part in hormone loss. During the time I was going through my depleted hormone crisis, I had the fortunate experience of hearing actress Suzanne Somers speak, and one of the important points she made was that hormone loss is no respecter of age or gender. Hormone deficiency can occur in anyone. I would recommend Suzanne's books to anyone interested in the subject of bioidentical hormones. I have read them and gleaned great insight from the experts Suzanne interviews and from her vast personal knowledge as well.

There are so many wonderful books and online reading materials that you can access to do your own research to help you make decisions regarding your health. The important thing I want to stress here is that it is *your* health, and it is *your* responsibility to research the medications you are taking and their side effects and those you would like to try. It is your responsibility to insist your doctor treat you with safe and, if you so choose, natural medications, or find a doctor who will.

The big controversy over bioidentical hormones and the fact that they have not been thoroughly tested in this country is an interesting issue to me. It seems that pharmaceutical companies will not spend the money to test natural products because they cannot generate as much income on products they cannot patent … not to mention how awful it would be for their business if we actually began treating our health issues instead of our symptoms.

I am going to send the thought and energy out to the universe for the companies who would benefit most financially from the general public becoming healthy to take on the challenge of financing tests on bioidentical hormones. It is my belief that the general public is too smart to continue to buy into all the drugs with their synthetic chemical cocktails and the corresponding side effects, especially the new generation … the dominoes are falling.

CHAPTER 18
THE BEGINNING OF WISDOM

THE NIGHT AFTER I FINISHED MY manuscript, I had the most wonderful dream I have ever had. I dreamed I was standing in the yard of a beautiful neighborhood that I had never seen before. Jace and Tiffany were small, around ten and six. They were playing on a lush, green lawn with huge trees that shaded the whole yard and even the street. A stranger walked up to me, a man around my age. We didn't speak. We didn't have to and instead just smiled.

I turned and walked out into the street; there was no traffic. In fact, everything was very still. Tiffany, Jace, and the man followed, and I began to dance. I danced up the street with my children, and the man following us was dancing as well. Next, I began to sing, actually more like a chant of joy. I sang the words, *I am glorious, glorious. You are wonderful, wonderful. I am glorious, glorious. You are wonderful, wonderful. I am glorious, glorious. You are wonderful, wonderful ...* My kids and the man began to sing too, and as we danced and sang down the street, I raised my arms in the air toward the heavens, and they swayed first to one side and then the other as we sang the chant.

Dancing, swaying, and singing, I looked up the street and saw coming toward us in the opposite direction a crowd of people, all types of people—all races, all ages, some in native dress, some in plain clothes. As they passed us, I would sway toward each of them and sing, *You are wonderful, wonderful ...* and each face would transform with a heavenly smile and a light so bright I could feel positive energy emitting from me to them and back again and then out to the whole universe. We danced and sang past hundreds of people, and when they had all gone by, I looked behind me. These hundreds of people had turned and were following us, singing and dancing to the same loving, healing, giving song—*I am glorious, glorious. You are wonderful, wonderful.*

And up ahead, lining both sides of the street, onlookers were clapping and waiting … waiting.

How many people in your life are waiting? Waiting for you to tell them how wonderful they are? The construction worker in Gilhooley's gave me the most powerful message of my life. "Our purpose here on earth is to send positive energy to each person we come in contact with." How many lives could you help change for the better with a positive word and a show of appreciation? Who in your world could be healed with your positive energy and outward expression of love? Do you need to express these feelings toward yourself? Love yourself. See the beautiful, wonderful person you are. Feel your creative ability to make a better world for yourself and others. You are powerful. Let your positive energy lift you up and radiate to others. You can change the world one person at a time, beginning with yourself.

It has been four years since I began *Hookers, Midgets, and Fire Trucks*. I have turned the big six-zero. The good news is that I feel like a thirty-year-old!

I continue to take bioidentical hormones. With every new person I meet, I am on a mission to help men and women know the importance of hormone balance and how it is a natural way to beat depression and many other age-related problems. I am not taking a single prescription medication other than hormones. I do not have an ache or pain. I experience zero menopausal symptoms, am allergy free, enjoy excellent energy, and feel so much joy. Oh, yes, and my sex drive is still through the roof!

Spiritually, I feel the presence of my guardians from the other side, and several times each day I speak out loud to them as if they were standing next to me in human form.

I am very happy to announce our family has been blessed with a bright and shining new soul, my precious grandson, Dalton Barrett, named after his uncle Jace Barrett. Both he and his big sister, Sky Olivia, and Tiffany, Chris, Kresta, and Micah, and so many amazing friends and family fill my life with love and laughter on a daily basis. I am so very blessed.

Yesterday, I sat on the back porch in my comfy, hanging rope swing, drinking coffee and watching the beauty of spring unfold in my tropical garden. My thoughts turned to how thankful I am for the wisdom I have attained through the pain and hard days. I thanked God for my joy and for my wonderful family and all the laughter we have shared. Visions of my precious granddaughter, Sky, flitted across my mind, and I marveled at what a special connection she and I have. I also saw Dalton, laughing and running with his arms outstretched to me, yelling, "Muggy!" (Muggy is the pet name Sky and Dalton have given me instead of Grandma). The thought of those two precious, tiny souls made me smile and feel so very happy.

I thanked my creator for my wonderful son-in-law and for my amazing daughter, who have been through so much with me. I threw kisses toward the sky and sent and received love from Jace and Mike and all those who have gone on before me. I thanked my maker for my two stepdaughters and prayed for their health to be restored and for their mom, Rita, to withstand her pain, worry, and the tough job she has as a caregiver. I thanked God for my mom, for Denise, and for all my wonderful friends who have stood steadfastly by me through everything. I sent positive energy to every person in the universe. And then I looked at the mixture of the lavender and purple in my hydrangeas and how the sunlight danced across the rich purple hues, and I began remembering a time over fifty years ago—and a little girl on her grandmother's front porch—and I thanked God again. I could just be the happiest person on earth.

• • • • •

LINDA'S LESSONS

We are all one, and no person is any more special than the next. All people experience joy and sorrow, and we are all learning lessons, whether we wish to or not. Every moment in your existence is a perfect part of your destiny—even those things that feel like mistakes. Be gentle with yourself and others. As the saying goes, most of us are doing the very best we can!

Remember, you are truly wonderful, no matter what your past

transgressions, because of the beautiful positive energy you have to share with all who pass your way.

If you have lost a loved one, I hope I have assured you that there is no *death*. The person you miss so much is with you always, as no one ever really dies. Welcome the messages they send your way, and revel in your ability to receive them. If you haven't heard or felt the person who has crossed over and you really need their reassurance, *ask*. And once you have asked, listen and watch for those signs. Don't suppose it to be a coincidence. *Know* it is their answer.

If age, life, or losses have plunged you into depression and you are unable to beat it alone, find a doctor who is willing to find the cause of your depression and treat the cause rather than the symptoms.

Listen to your soul. Your internal guidance system will never steer you wrong. Every one of us has an eternally wise support system within and guides on the other side pulling for us. Listen and respond only to that natural compass, your soul. Though family and friends love you and want the best for you, no one knows the answer but you.

Hookers, Midgets, and Fire Trucks has been a story about me and my life, but it was you and your life I was hoping to impact. Our family was not perfect by Emily Post's standards. We were not politically correct. My guess is that your family has imperfections too. We were a family of extremes: live hard, work hard, play hard, and die with no regrets. You may have chosen a different path. It's all good. It is all unfolding as it should. We are all headed in the same direction. Jace really did say to every person he invited to a party, "Come on, there's going to be hookers, midgets, and fire trucks!" because he believed in people, all people, and the goodness of their journey.

Thank you so much for spending your valuable time with me. As I write this, I am sending so much love and positive energy to you.

I am glorious, glorious. You are wonderful, wonderful.

RESOURCES

Hotze, Stephen F., MD. *Hormones, Health, and Happiness: A Natural Formula for Rediscovering Youth with Bioidentical Hormones.* New York, NY: Warner Wellness, Hatchette Book Groups, USA, 2005.

Newton, Michael. *Journey of Souls.* St. Paul, MN: Llewellyn Publications, 1994, 1996.

O'Neill, Kim. *How to Talk with Your Angels.* New York, NY: Avon Books, 1995. http://www.kimoneillpsychic.com/

Somers, Suzanne. http://www.suzannesomers.com/

To my husband, Mike:
This book is of course written for you, my darling husband, my
Don Quixote, dreamer of impossible dreams, my Michael Don
Thompson (Buggy). Thank you so much for all the lessons you
taught me, and for making me a better me. I will always love you.

To my daughter, Tiffany Lynn:
Words cannot begin to express my love and appreciation to you for being
Mike's and my best friend; for how unbelievably strong you were when
Jace died; and now, for being the best mom on earth for Sky Olivia and
Dalton Barrett. You are wonderful. I love you, and I am so proud of you!

To my son, Jace Barrett:
My darling son, you made laughter a constant companion in my life.
I think we did okay this time around. I love and miss you so much.

To Micah and Kresta:
Thank you for allowing your "stepmonster" to love you,
for loving me, and for being the warriors you are.